Lois Webb

The Gifts Of The Holy Spirit Are For You

Dr. Carol J. Robeson

Shiloh Publishing House
P.O. Box 100; Woodburn, OR 97071
carol6077@yahoo.com
(800) 607-6195

THE GIFTS OF THE HOLY SPIRIT
ARE FOR YOU

Author - Dr. Carol J. Robeson
Published by Shiloh Publishing House
© Copyright 2002 by Shiloh Publishing House

ISBN# 1-891879-12-X

All scripture is quoted from the King James Version.

Cover Photo: Deception Pass, Washington
by Dr. Jerry Robeson

Shiloh Publishing House
P.O. Box 100; Woodburn, OR 97071
(800) 607-6195
carol6077@yahoo.com

All rights reserved except for use in reviews, this publication may not be reproduced, stored or transmitted in any form, or by any means mechanical or electronic, photocoypying, recording or otherwise without prior written permission of the author.

PREFACE

God has been calling mankind since the Garden of Eden when He was searching for Adam to present himself in the cool of the evening for fellowship (Genesis 3:8-10). Adam hid himself because of his sin and subsequent fear of God. God continues calling individuals even when He knows where they are hiding out of fear because of their sin and rebellion. He does not drag anybody involuntarily out of hiding; He patiently calls to them until they respond of their own desire to know Him.

Throughout history God has called people to become prophets, kings and priests. These callings used to be for just a few in the Old Testament. That scenario changed when Jesus came; now He calls each person individually to enjoy his rights and privileges as a child of God.

The calling of God is a permanent status. Once Saul, David and Solomon were anointed to become the kings of Israel, they were in the office for the duration of their lifetime. David was aware of this and would not allow harm to come to Saul because of the anointing and call God had placed on his life for the office of king.

David and his son Solomon both had their times of error while serving as king of Israel. However, the calling of the office of king and the anointing that went with it was theirs.

We see from this that the calling and anointing of God don't in themselves make a sinless life. The person must still choose to serve God on a daily basis to have the continued benefits of God's direction. A king without any plans is not a good leader of his people.

God chose Aaron, Eli and Samuel as priests to serve Him. These were spiritual callings and anointings that endured for the lifetime of the person. God calls us to be priests to him for our entire lifetime. It isn't something one tries and throws aside when he gets tired of it. It should be more exciting each day for that person to come into the presence of God for service.

The prophets of God were called directly to be His mouth-pieces. They were to speak the words of God to others as if God Himself were doing the talking. Some were chosen for this even from their mother's womb. God called others by name to fulfill His important election. Every believer is called and commanded to speak the words of God everywhere and make disciples. This calling should carry the full significance intended for it. True believers should have a desire to proclaim the Word of God at every given opportunity.

It is impossible to adequately describe the exact ways or means God uses to call a person because He tailors the call to fit each individual. The gifts God gives can be described by their rules of use and function, but they must be experienced for full comprehension.

Without experiencing salvation on a personal basis, a person is very much like a banker with money all around him that he can see and keep account of, but having none in his own personal bank account to spend. He could be penniless, although he was surrounded with wealth that belongs to others.

God has given each person a calling and a heavenly account to draw on that is abundant with gifts and power. It is up to the individual to take the time to become so personally acquainted with the giver of these gifts that each gift is unfolded in his life at the appropriate time and setting.

Neither the gifts nor the calling of God can be earned or won as a prize for good deeds or behavior. They flow continuously from the liberal heart of God the Father, Son and Holy Spirit. He is not prejudiced in his gifts and calling against men, women, slave, free, Greek or Hebrew, educated or uneducated. In the things of the Spirit, all people are the same in Jesus Christ (Gal. 3:28).

Table of Contents

List of Illustrations

DEDICATION

I dedicate this work to my two beautiful daughters and their husbands who have blessed me with four of the most wonderful, intelligent, gorgeous, grandchildren a person could possibly have. (All truth...No predjudice here!).

I also dedicate this to Ruth Friesen, my good friend and ministry partner since my husband, Jerry, went to be with the Lord. Jesus sent His workers out two by two and when He found us two widows, He sent us to the far corners of the world to minister. Ruth, a wonderful teacher and minister herself, encouraged me to continue writing and teaching when I thought I might just sit down and smell the flowers. To God be the Glory!

Dr. Carol J. Robeson

Diagram 1.1

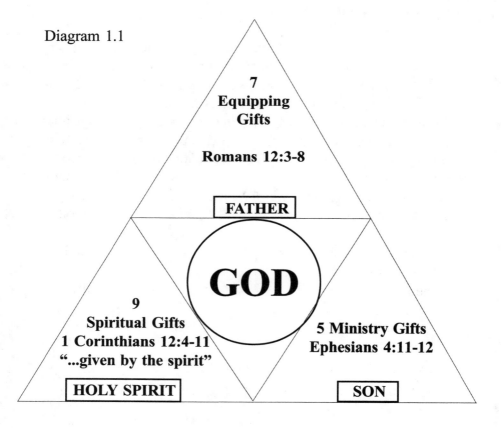

7
Equipping
Gifts

Romans 12:3-8

FATHER

GOD

9
Spiritual Gifts
1 Corinthians 12:4-11
"...given by the spirit"

5 Ministry Gifts
Ephesians 4:11-12

HOLY SPIRIT

SON

INTRODUCTION

God calls, confirms and sets in motion each person's spiritual journey when they recieve Him as their Lord and Savior. It is abundantly evident from scripture that God delights in giving people gifts who choose to follow Him. People in spiritual authority may impart gifts or blessings but it is always God who is ultimately the gift giver, not the person who symbolically places his hands on another person.

Diagram 1.1, shows the relationship of the triune God and the specific gifts that each gives to the Body of Christ. This study will show the relationship of how each person is individually called by God and then given supernatural gifts from the Holy Spirit to help make that calling become a reality and an effective blessing to the whole Church.

Three triangles within a larger triangle represent the three major gift packages mentioned in the Bible. The center circle within the large triangle is labeled **God** and represents the trinity of God in three persons, the Father, the Son, and the Holy Spirit. Each person of the Godhead has gifts and callings to give a believer as he makes his spiritual journey. The person is not usually aware of all these gifts at the outset of his walk with the Lord. They are revealed and developed as the person continues to grow in his spiritual

THE GIFTS OF THE HOLY SPIRIT ARE FOR YOU!

understanding and faithful obedience to God.

In the small triangle on the top of illustration 1.1, the seven motivational gifts are illustrated. These are given by God, the Father.

"For I say, through the grace given unto me, to every man that is among you, not to think of himself more highly than he ought to think; but to think soberly, according as God hath dealt to every man the measure of faith. For as we have many members in one body, and all members have not the same office: So we, being many, are one body in Christ, and every one members one of another. Having then gifts differing according to the grace that is given to us, whether prophecy, let us prophesy according to the proportion of faith; Or ministry, let us wait on our ministering: or he that teacheth, on teaching; Or he that exhorteth, on exhortation: he that giveth, let him do it with simplicity; he that ruleth, with diligence; he that sheweth mercy, with cheerfulness." (Romans 12:3-8)

When a person is spiritually born into the Body of Christ, each of these motivational gifts should be evident, but one will usually be more prevalent than the others. When a study is made of these gifts, people can understand more clearly where each fits into the Body of Christ. A thorough study of the gifts should also promote patience and appreciation of other people who have differing gifts.

The lower right corner triangle contains information about the five-fold ministry gifts that pertain to the full-time ministry callings. Jesus gave these gifts to the Church for the perfecting of the Saints. "And he [Jesus] gave some, apostles; and some, prophets; and some, evangelists; and some, pastors and teachers; For the perfecting of the saints, for the work of the ministry, for the edifying of the body of Christ:" (Ephesians 4:11,12)

The lower left corner triangle contains information about the nine spiritual gifts found in 1 Corinthians 12, given by the Holy Spirit. These nine gifts divide easily into three groups of three each. There are three spoken gifts, three power gifts and three revelation gifts. "For to one is given by the Spirit the word of wisdom; to another the word of knowledge by the same Spirit; to another faith by the same Spirit; to another the gifts of healing by the same Spirit; to another the working of miracles; to another prophecy; to another discerning of spirits; to another divers kinds of tongues; to another

2

the interpretation of tongues:" (1 Corinthians 12:8-10)

It is very carefully explained to the readers of 1 Corinthians that these gifts are, "...given by the spirit," (v. 7), "...as he (the Spirit) wills" (v. 11).

Around each of the three minor triangles and the outer perimeter of the larger triangle a starred line is placed that would display the rightful place of the fruit of the Spirit.

"But the fruit of the Spirit is love, joy, peace, longsuffering, gentleness, goodness, faith, Meekness, temperance: against such there is no law." (Galatians 5:22, 23)

It is very important that the fruit of the Spirit are present and growing in the believer's life. The absence of them makes the gifts become nothing more than a loud, useless, clanging noise (I Corinthians 13:1). The apostle Paul said, "This I say, walk in the Spirit, and ye shall not fulfill the lust of the flesh" (Galatians 5:16) This passage draws a clear distinction between the life of one who is walking in the Spirit and the life of one who is walking in the flesh. If we then are to judge a person by the fruit of the Spirit that is present or absent, this is an essential part of the study to discern more clearly who will inherit the kingdom of God in spite of the calling of God or even gifts that might have been evident.

This book will investigate only the later grouping of spiritual gifts given by the Holy Spirit. Diagram 1.2, on the following page, displays their three major categories.

**"He that sows to the spirit shall of
the spirit reap life everlasting..."
Galatians 6:8**

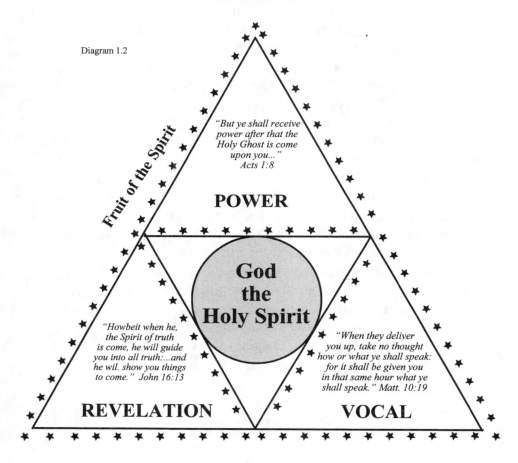

Diagram 1.2

Fruit of the Spirit

*"But ye shall receive
power after that the
Holy Ghost is come
upon you..."
Acts 1:8*

POWER

**God
the
Holy Spirit**

*"Howbeit when he,
the Spirit of truth
is come, he will guide
you into all truth:...and
he wil. show you things
to come." John 16:13*

*"When they deliver
you up, take no thought
how or what ye shall speak:
for it shall be given you
in that same hour what ye
shall speak." Matt. 10:19*

REVELATION

VOCAL

**"For he whom God hath sent speaketh the
words [Rhema] of God: for God giveth not
the Spirit by measure unto him."
John 3:34**

CHAPTER 1

THE HOLY SPIRIT

The Holy Spirit, the third person of the Trinity, is co-equal and co-eternal with God the Father and God the Son (the Lord Jesus Christ). (Acts 5:3-4; 13:2; 21:11) *"For there are three that bear record in heaven, the Father, the Word, and the Holy Ghost: and these three are one."* (I John 5:7)

The Holy Spirit is the Helper whom the Father sent to be with the Church after Christ ascended into heaven. (John 14:16-17) He now resides on earth in each believer. *"And there are three that bear witness in earth, the spirit, and the water, and the blood: and these three agree in one."* (I John 5:8)

The presence of the Holy Spirit living in a person creates yet another dynamic that we can refer to as, "God's anointing" on a person. It will be there to a greater or lesser degree depending on each believer's intimacy and relationship with the Holy Spirit. The personal desire of each individual to press in quickly and obediently to the anointing of God in part determines the response of the Holy Spirit's anointing in their life.

We can all travel to the seashore and sit in the sand while watching the tide flow in and out for hours. There are many people who are totally satisfied with that experience. However, there are others who kick their shoes off and want to feel the soft sand and maybe even venture to walk up to the water's edge and enjoy the thrill and refreshing of the wet sand under their feet. Still others roll up their pant-legs or hitch up their skirts so the shallow waters can be enjoyed. Then last, but not least, are those who come ready to dive in head first or launch out into the deep away from the shore line where they can enjoy a depth and perspective totally unknown by the spectators and shore-waders.

These are the people God's Holy Spirit is looking for so He can pour out His anointing on them. They know they're over their head each time they venture out but their faith to float is in the Lord.

Can they become ship-wrecked? Yes, as soon as they take their eyes off Jesus and begin to look to their own strength and understanding, they begin to sink.

Jesus said it would be better for Him to leave this earth and for the Holy Spirit to come in His place.

"And I will pray the Father, and he shall give you another Comforter, that he may abide with you for ever; Even the Spirit of truth; whom the world cannot receive, because it seeth him not, neither knoweth him: but ye know him; for he dwelleth with you, and shall be in you." (John 14:16,17)

"Nevertheless I tell you the truth; It is expedient for you that I go away: for if I go not away, the Comforter will not come unto you; but if I depart, I will send him unto you." (John 16:7)

Jesus is the baptizer in the Holy Spirit today. Every believer is encouraged by Jesus himself to be filled with the Spirit.

"I indeed baptize you with water unto repentance: but he that cometh after me is mightier than I, whose shoes I am not worthy to bear: he shall baptize you with the Holy Ghost, and with fire:" (Matthew 3:11)

"I indeed have baptized you with water: but he shall baptize you with the Holy Ghost." (Mark 1:8)

"And be not drunk with wine, wherein is excess; but be filled with the Spirit;" (Ephesians 5:18)

There is only one Holy Spirit, He is also known as the Spirit of adoption who convicts of sin and draws a person to salvation. *"For ye have not received the spirit of bondage again to fear; but ye have received the Spirit of adoption, whereby we cry, Abba, Father"* (Romans 8:15).

One in The Spirit

The Holy Spirit joins with the spirit of the believer when the person accepts Christ as their personal Savior. They become inter-twined like a rope is for strength and become as one. The Holy Spirit continues to be the believer's intercessor throughout his Christian life. He instructs, illuminates, empowers, and uses the believer who yields to God's will. *"But he that is joined unto the Lord is one spirit."* (I Corinthians 6:17)

The Holy Spirit takes up permanent residence in the life of the believer at the moment of salvation. Although the ministry of the Spirit is limited by disobedience, He does not leave unless He is totally rejected and grieved.

The human body becomes the temple of the Holy Spirit that also houses the person's own spirit. *"Know ye not that ye are the temple of God, and that the Spirit of God dwells in you?"* (I Corinthians 3:16; 6:19)

Daniel identified the location of his spirit as being in the center part of his body. According to scripture, our bodies become the temples where both our spirit and God's Spirit live together. *"I Daniel was grieved in my spirit in the midst of my body."* (Daniel 7:15)

Therefore when God's Spirit enters a person at salvation He takes up residence with their spirit and as Romans 8:12 and 14 in-structs: *"For as many as are led by the Spirit of God, they are the sons of God." "The Spirit itself beareth witness with our spirit, that we are the children of God:"*

When God wants to get a person's attention, all He has to do is nudge his spirit with the Holy Spirit that lives in him. Whenever God wants to tell him something or communicate with him, He will start by stimulating, or bearing witness with, the man's spirit first. This is an important factor when a person begins to respond to the gifts and anointing of the Holy Spirit because God first of all gets their atten-tion in the spirit before He does anything else. This process brings a confirmation that it really is God at work and not a desire of the flesh or any outside influence trying to use him.

Jesus said in John 10:27, *"My sheep hear my voice, and I know them, and they follow me:"* It is very important to develop the spiri-tual ears of one's spirit to hear and recognize the voice of God. This passage instructs people that those who hear the shepherd's voice will not be fooled by an impostor. Satan is the great deceiver and tries to play mind games with people. Only the Holy Spirit living in a believer can witness or speak to their spirit, therefore all other voices come from outside sources or the person's own thoughts, and contend for the mind.

The Gifts of the Holy Spirit

The spiritual gifts of the Holy Spirit are extra benefits added to one's relationship with Jesus. They are not to be mistaken for God-given talents.

"And there are differences of administrations, but the same Lord. And there are diversities of operations, but it is the same God which worketh all in all. But the manifestation of the Spirit is given to every man to profit withal: for to one is given by the Spirit the word of wisdom, to another the word of knowledge by the same Spirit; to another faith by the same Spirit; to another the gifts of healing by the same Spirit; to another the working of miracles; to another prophecy; to another discerning of spirits; to another divers kinds of tongues; to another the interpretation of tongues: But all these worketh that one and the selfsame Spirit, dividing to every man severally as He will." (1 Corinthians 12:5-11)

It should be noted that scripture instructs all things to be done in an orderly manner concerning the operation and use of spiritual gifts. (I Corinthians 14:40)

Spiritual Graces

The nine spiritual gifts or "graces" are all given by the Holy Spirit. The word, "charismatic" (taken from the Greek, *charismata* in 1 Corinthians 12:4) is used to describe these supernatural gifts given by the grace, favor, or special kindness of the Holy Spirit to believers. Someone defined charismata as: "gifts given to us in spite of the fact we do not deserve them."

People do not own these gifts. They are the property of the Holy Spirit. He distributes them at His will for specific needs and occasions. When there is a proper understanding of spiritual gifts, God will do new things each day and there will not be a need for people to look at the past and expect a rerun of yesterday's experiences.

God uses people in spite of their education, or lack of it. He also uses them in spite of their background, or their variety of experiences.

"In connection with this common ministry, each person has a distinctive role to fulfill: 'to each one is given the manifestation of the Spirit.' The common good is the orientation of the gifts of the Spirit, and to that end each person in the community is involved. Accordingly, in a spiritually gifted community, people should not look to one person or to a few to minister. Rather they should look to the Lord, expecting Him to minister by the Spirit through any and all who are present." (Williams, J. Rodman,1992, p. 27.)

Believers are instructed to desire spiritual gifts from the Holy Spirit and not try to shut them off. *"Covet earnestly the best gifts and yet he shall show unto you a more excellent way,"* which is love mentioned in chapter 13 of 1 Corinthians. All the gifts should be motivated by love for others or they become, *"sounding brass, or a tinkling cymbal."* (I Corinthians 13:1)

It is important that each person be submitted to the rest of the Body of Christ to use the gifts of the Spirit properly. Balance comes through submission to each other. Seasoned believers in the Word of God should be present to observe and judge the activities of the Holy Spirit when He is active in group meetings. *"Let the prophets speak two or three, and let the other judge."* (I Corinthians 14:29)

In the Old Testament and the ministry of Jesus seven of these nine spiritual gifts were operational. The day of Pentecost, with the outpouring of the Holy Spirit on men and women, brought the arrival of two more gifts. The gifts of speaking in tongues and interpretation of tongues were given to benefit the New Testament Church.

God's New Testament Church Plan

God set the New Testament Church in order just once. He does not change His mind and redo His design every few hundred years to conform to man's changing world. Whenever the Church loses the manifestations of her gifts she becomes anemic, neutralized and altogether different from what God's original plan for her was. God's plan is to keep His Church alive and exciting so people will be drawn to it because it is the only light in this dismal world's disintegrating system.

THE GIFTS OF THE HOLY SPIRIT ARE FOR YOU!

Through the years of history, the gifts of the Holy Spirit have been largely neglected. As a result, the Church lost much of its power that was in evidence during the apostolic period. A study of history clearly shows however, that there have always been remnant groups of people who have valued and kept the gifts of the Spirit alive.

During the nineteenth and twentieth centuries the gifts of the Spirit became a source of untold blessing to millions of people as they were rediscovered and restored worldwide in the Body of Christ. Yet, they remain a point of consternation to others whose doctrinal renderings have them convinced that God does not empower His Church in this fashion anymore.

How it is possible that the gifts of the Spirit could have been virtually lost to the Church for so many years? Whenever there is a lack of emphasis given to the power of the Word of God and works of God, they can become dormant. For hundreds of years the truth of justification by faith was set aside and not until the days of Martin Luther did people declare again this unshakable Biblical truth. They were stirred to search the scriptures for the truth of God's Word and realized their lack. The reformers of history have always found that all of God's rich gifts and callings were set in the Church to prosper the Body of Christ until He returns.

The gifts of the Spirit were not only given to benefit the clergy, they were put in the Church and made available to every person as the Holy Spirit chooses to use them. Each believer can become aware of their place in the Body of Christ and how God wants to use them by studying the Word of God and developing a close communion with the person of the Holy Spirit.

CHAPTER 2

THE DOORWAY TO THE HOLY SPIRIT'S GIFTS

The recognized doorway to full manifestation of spiritual gifts in the lives of individuals is through the baptism of the Holy Spirit accompanied by what is popularly known as a personal prayer language or speaking in tongues. This was sent on Pentecost to the waiting believers in Jerusalem.

"And when the day of Pentecost was fully come, they were all with one accord in one place. And suddenly there came a sound from heaven as of a rushing mighty wind, and it filled all the house where they were sitting. And there appeared unto them cloven tongues like as of fire, and it sat upon each of them. And they were all filled with the Holy Ghost, and began to speak with other tongues, as the Spirit gave them utterance." (Acts 2:1-4)

The word baptism means "immersion, or to be completely covered by"; i.e., to be baptized with the Holy Spirit means to be immersed or filled with the Spirit. (A Critical Lexicon and Concordance to the English and Greek New Testament, p. 80, 1979).

The early Church believers all had a vital personal experience when they were baptized by the Holy Spirit. They knew when He came, where He came, and how He came. When Paul asked the Ephesian believers if they had received the Holy Spirit since they had believed, he was not referring to a doctrine, he was referring to an experience. When he found that they had not received the Holy

Spirit, he immediately challenged them to experience it. The result was that they spoke in tongues and prophesied in Acts 19:2.

Jesus said, one sign that would follow believers would be speaking in new tongues (Mark 16:17). That was fulfilled when believers in Christ were baptized in the Holy Spirit and spoke with tongues: *"And they were **all** filled with the Holy Ghost, and began to speak with other tongues, as the Spirit gave them utterance."* (Acts 2:4)

*"And they of the circumcision which believed were astonished, as many as came with Peter, because that on the Gentiles also was poured out the gift of the Holy Ghost. For they heard them speak with tongues and magnify God." (*Acts 10:45-46)

"And when Paul had laid his hands upon them, the Holy Ghost came on them; and they spake with tongues, and prophesied." (Acts 19:6)

Speaking in tongues is the only known consistent evidence scripture gives showing people were baptized in the Holy Spirit. This beautiful manner of communication with God is available to all who want to be baptized in the Holy Spirit.

The Bible says in II Corinthians 13:1, *"in the mouth of two or three witnesses every word shall be established."* Since we have three clear scriptures (Acts 2:4; 10:46; 19:6), this evidence of tongues can readily be established.

Paul the Apostle wanted all Christians to speak in tongues and was grateful to God that he spoke in tongues more than anyone in the Corinthian Church (I Corinthians 14:5,18). Paul was speaking of the devotional tongues that all can experience in personal worship and intercession before God.

People are not directed anywhere in the Bible to seek to speak in tongues. Instead believers are challenged to receive the baptism in the Holy Spirit. When Jesus baptizes us in the Holy Spirit we are given the ability to speak in an unknown tongue to God. God, however wants us to seek Him for the fullness of the Holy Spirit, not just for tongues.

"And I say unto you, Ask, and it shall be given you; seek, and ye shall find; knock, and it shall be opened unto you. For every one that asketh receiveth; and he that seeketh findeth; and to him that knocketh it shall be opened. If a son shall ask bread of any of you that is a

father, will he give him a stone? or if he ask a fish, will he for a fish give him a serpent? Or if he shall ask an egg, will he offer him a scorpion? If ye then, being evil, know how to give good gifts unto your children: how much more shall your heavenly Father give the Holy Spirit to them that ask him?" (Luke 11:9-13)

The Holy Spirit wants the freedom to express Himself through each individual. The initial outpouring of His Spirit in the lives of people encourages them to go deeper into the mysteries of God. Resident in the Holy Spirit are the nine spiritual gifts He will use when a need arises.

The spiritual gifts are ways that God shows His mighty power to the individual and the Body of Christ. The focus of the Holy Spirit is always on the Lordship of Christ, and always exalts Him.

THE GIFTS OF THE HOLY SPIRIT ARE FOR YOU!

CHAPTER 3

PHYSICAL MANIFESTATIONS AND THE HOLY SPIRIT

At ball games I've noticed many things go on that are not classified as playing football, basketball or even baseball. People scream, shout, jump, etc. but these have nothing to do with the ballgame rules. However, all these activities are legitimate results of enthusiasm at a ball game.

Dancing, shouting, crying, shaking, laughing or running while enjoying the outpouring of the Holy Spirit is not necessarily a manifestation of the Holy Spirit. They are not gifts. They are human reactions to the power and majesty of God's presence touching human flesh when the Holy Spirit is operative. On the other hand, some people have no reaction at all. It can be honestly said that the work of the Holy Spirit is not dependent on whether a person does or does not feel something. Any physical reaction we have while enjoying the presence of the Holy Spirit is not necessarily the Spirit of God, but more often, natural individual human responses. In becoming knowledgeable about spiritual gifts people must learn to distinguish between human reactions and the genuine working of the Holy Spirit.

In recent years there has been a great emphasis placed on physical manifestations such as falling on the floor or laughing uncontrollably. If these reactions are carried to an extreme they can be a real hinderance to other sincere seekers who are just entering into this type of experience. They are not especially wrong, but they are very inconsiderate of others at times. It could be likened to going to a nice restraunt and having someone at a neighboring table laugh and talk so loudly that you can't hear the one you came with speak to you. It can be rude and crude at best if carried too far.

Periodically throughout history the same reaction of people to God's Power has brought cleansing, refreshing and refurnishing in His Church for further service. These same reactions usually ushered in times of revival and awakening as people experienced or observed these manifestations. Sometimes these activities loosen people up, humbles them under the mighty hand of God and then serves to get their minds off themselves and focus their whole attention on the Lordship of Christ.

Commanding Our Attention

Neither Paul nor God wanted believers to be ignorant of spiritual truths. Six times in the New Testament Paul said, *"brethren, I would not have you ignorant."* One thing He did not want us to be ignorant about is the spiritual gifts given to all born-again believers.

God said, *"My people perish for lack of knowledge."* (Hosea 4:6)

Paul took it on himself to write to the Corinthian church the things that God had revealed to him about spiritual gifts. *"If any man think himself to be a prophet or spiritual, let him acknowledge that the things that I write to you are the commandments of the Lord."* (I Corinthians 14:37)

If these were the commandments of the Lord for the people in Paul's day, then they are still the commandments of the Lord for today. God wants us to learn these same teachings and use them as guidelines.

When a person is honestly being used by the Holy Spirit, he will not do anything that will blaspheme the Name of Jesus nor say things contrary to the Word of God.

Spiritual Gifts Convince People

We are all aware that Jesus showed signs and wonders throughout His ministry to get people to hear the Gospel. The first miracle of

16

turning water into wine at the wedding in Cana of Galilee was done for this purpose. *"This beginning of signs Jesus did in Cana of Galilee, and manifested His glory; and His disciples believed in Him."* (John 2:11)

Through this, it can be seen why the gifts of the Spirit and especially miracles are such a necessity to the world and the Body of Christ. They make believers out of doubters. Paul was a great advocate of this approach, *"And my speech and my preaching was not with enticing words of man's wisdom, but in demonstration of the Spirit and of power."*: (I Corinthians 2:4)

The gifts solidified Paul's ministry in the eyes of observers. People watch ministries to see if their words are confirmed by a demonstration of the power of God. When they see God's power in operation they know that ministry has the approval of God on it.

For twenty years in Latin America we were involved in open-air, divine healing crusades. Some asked why we did not just have salvation crusades and later tell them about healing. The people already had religions of their own and churches to attend so they were not interested in hearing another sermon delivered without power. The only power they had ever seen was the power of the devil through occult practices. We wanted them to hear something followed by God's divine power in signs and wonders afterwards so they could never forget or dispute the source. Each night became a Mt. Carmel experience on the platform as the people watched to see what would happen that night.

My husband, Jerry, set up the crusade sites on empty lots, usually facing busy bus routes. He strung up lights, put up a rustic platform and preached a simple Gospel message every night. When people saw the crusades, they would come, listen and see God doing wonderful things each night. They were told that if they wanted healing they must first accept the Healer as their Lord and Savior. Most of them needed healing, so that became the hook in their jaw to bring them in. After they accepted the Lord, God healed them and did thoroughly life-changing miracles in each crusade. People told their friends and relatives about what they had seen and testimonies were run daily on radio and television programs so in a few months there developed a strong new church with hundreds of enthusiastic believers that multiplied daily into solid congregations of two, four and ten thousand people.

Spiritual Gifts Edify Believers.

Every believer is encouraged to improve himself in the use of the gifts so the whole Body of Christ may be edified, exhorted and comforted. The gifts of the Spirit are personal, and also, corporal. They are for the each person in the Body of Christ.

"But he that prophesieth speaketh unto men to edification, and exhortation, and comfort. Even so ye, forasmuch as ye are zealous of spiritual gifts, seek that ye may excel to the edifying of the church. How is it then brethren? when ye come together, every one of you hath a psalm, hath a doctrine, hath a tongue, hath a revelation, hath an interpretation. Let all things be done unto edifying. If any man speak in an unknown tongue, let it be by two, or at the most by three, and that by course; and let one interpret." (I Corinthians 14:3,12,26,27)

Spiritual Gifts Demonstrate God's Power.

Paul recognized how fruitless his long theological words were that he had spent a life time learning at the feet of the best scholars of his day. Paul would probably be a college professor today or possibly a highly paid mind at NASA. However, he gave way to the Holy Spirit to guide him and display the power of God. He set aside all the high sounding terms he had learned and spoke with a simple message, just as Jesus did. He was a communicator and God blessed the results with signs following and allowed him to write more of the New Testament than any other author.

When the gospel message is kept simple, it will always attract the unbeliever and teach the believer exactly what the Holy Spirit wants. When the Holy Spirit anoints simple truths, they become deep doctrinal insights to the hearers of the Word and the anointing will be followed with the supernatural that mankind craves to experience.

Spiritual Gifts Are to Evangelize the World.

Jesus prophesied several times about the outpouring of the Holy Spirit, *"But you shall receive power when the Holy Spirit is come upon you; and you shall be witnesses to Me in Jerusalem, and in all Judea and Samaria, and to the end of the earth."* (Acts 1:8)

At Pentecost God opened the doors to believers to preach the gospel to the ends of the earth. Today, He has entrusted the tools of the gospel into our hands through radio, television and the printed page to do incredible things while getting the message out to the ends of the earth. We can send missionaries out and supply them with vehicles to get into the most remote areas to preach the Word. Via the satellite and the computer information highway the gospel is being spread to every nation, tribe and tongue faster than any previous period in history. This is truly a day when the prophecy is being fulfilled in greater measure than ever before and it is a privilege to be a participant as nations are constantly opening to the Gospel around the world.

Peter and Paul would have given anything to live today with all the conveniences and methods of preaching the gospel. Satellite television has changed the face of the ministry forever. A person can reach more people in one broadcast than most individuals can in a lifetime of ministry. This is a powerful last-day witness of God's power and glory to the world.

In Mark 16, Jesus said signs would follow those that believe. Why would signs follow them? So they could evangelize the world. Jesus told them they were to go into all the world and preach the gospel to every creature and he that believeth would be saved. One of the signs was believers would lay hands on the sick and they would recover. In His name they would cast out devils. If they drank any deadly thing, it would not hurt them. He also said that they would speak with new tongues.

The first disciples and apostles took Jesus at His word. They began to teach and speak all over their known world. The result was, *"They went forth preaching everywhere, the Lord working with them and confirming the word with signs following."* (Mark 16:20)

God will always confirm His Word with signs following. It never returns void. He will never leave or forsake a person when they speak His Word to any situation. We must take the message to our generation and fulfill His command. We are not weak or powerless. On the contrary, He has given us all of His power to back us up.

God's greatest desire in any of the gift areas is that we grow into the full stature that He has designed for us. He wants to embolden us to bless the Body of Christ, witness, and bring new ones into the life of salvation that He has prepared for us. (Acts 2:13; 4:13; 4:29; 4:31; 5:28)

Spiritual Gifts Perfect the Church and Establish Believers.

Spiritual gifts are given to believers to help establish them. *"For I long to see you that I may impart to you some spiritual gift to the end that you may be established"* (Romans 1:11).

Supernatural manifestations are living reminders that God is alive. We're not commemorating a dead god carved of wood or stone that cannot respond to needs. God is alive and well.

Paul placed a strong emphasis on teaching and exercising spiritual gifts so people would be free in the use of them and become more established. The Holy Spirit was sent to indwell each believer and guide him into all truth. *"Howbeit when he, the Spirit of truth is come, he will guide you into all truth: for he shall not speak of himself; but whatsoever he shall hear, that shall he speak: and he will show you things to come"* (John 16:13).

When people get sound teaching on spiritual gifts they are not afraid to move into them because their faith increases and they begin to naturally reach out for more of God's blessings and greater anointings. Fear steps aside, and by faith individuals give a prophecy or an interpretation of tongues. Faith speaks miracles into motion and moves mountains.

Spiritual Gifts Are for Spiritual Profit.

Spiritual gifts are for spiritual profit. We can grow wealthy in spiritual things. The wealth God offers, supersedes any amount of financial wealth that can be accumulated in a lifetime. *"But the mani-*

festation of the Spirit is given to every man to profit withal."(I Corinthians 12:7)

The Holy Spirit came to benefit everyone mutually in the Body of Christ. Heavenly communication with God, while praying in other tongues, can be effectively used to intercede for personal needs as well as the needs of others (Romans 8:26; I Corinthians 14:2, 4; Jude 20). Through spiritual intercession needs are met, bodies are healed and souls are set free from the destroyer. "*But seek ye first the kingdom of God, and his righteousness; and all these things shall be added unto you*" (Matthew 6:33).

He Came to Reprove the World of Sin

The Holy Spirit came to reprove the world of sin, righteousness and judgment.

Nevertheless I tell you the truth; It is expedient for you that I go away: for if I go not away, the Comforter will not come unto you; but if I depart, I will send him unto you. And when he is come, he will reprove the world of sin, and of righteousness, and of judgment: Of Sin, because they believe not on me; Of righteousness, because I go to my Father, and ye see me no more; Of judgment, because the prince of this world is judged (John 16:7-11).

Use The Gifts In Obedience to The Holy Spirit

The gifts of the Spirit are always used in obedience to the Holy Spirit. He not only gives them, He directs how they should be used. "*But all these work, and the selfsame spirit dividing to every man severally as he wills*" (1 Corinthians 12:11).

The Holy Spirit assigns to each person the workings of the gifts of the Spirit as He sees necessary. When a need arises for a gift of the Spirit to be in operation, the Holy Spirit may use anyone to deliver that gift if they make themselves available. The Holy Spirit living in them decides their availability and what gift would best meet the need of the situation. One day He may use a person to pray for healing and another day to deliver a Word of Knowledge or discern a spirit that is not from God.

Every person can be used by the Holy Spirit. When one is born into the Body of Christ, the moment they accept Jesus into their life, the Holy Spirit comes in to live. When a need arises, if He sees that the believer is willing to let Him use them, the Holy Spirit will not hesitate to call on them with a gift or combination of gifts. He stirs the human spirit into action when the person dares to throw away their self consciousness and move with His gentle urging into God consciousness.

Do not limit God. The potential of all nine gifts is in each Christian and over a period of time any one of them may be manifest in life situations or ministry to people.

Some people have mistakenly limited their usefulness to God because someone has laid hands on them and told them they have a *"gift of healing."* They do not. They have the Holy Spirit. In Him are all nine gifts of the Spirit, one of them is healing. Believers don't receive just one gift—they receive them all through the Holy Spirit. He chooses which one will meet a particular need. A person only needs to be available to be used by the Holy Spirit.

Use the Gifts In Love

"Though I speak with the tongues of men and of angels, and have not love, I am as a sounding brass and a tinkling cymbal." (I Corinthians 13:1)

A believer may be used by the Spirit to manifest any of the nine gifts of the Spirit from time to time. However, if love and the other fruit of the Spirit are not evident in their life they will hinder those who are receiving the results of the gifts because their attitudes will be bad. *"Follow after love and desire spiritual gifts."* (1 Corinthians 14:1) We're instructed to want spiritual gifts in our lives and at the same time demonstrate love.

Why is love so important? The Word of God teaches that God is love. He not only has love, but love flows out of Him to all His creation. He is the fountain out of which all real love flows here on earth.

If we're going to demonstrate God's power and mercy then we need to be a part of that love relationship. *"Beloved, let us love one another for love is of God and everyone that loves is born of God and knows God."* (1 John 4:7)

"And we have known and believed the love that God has to us, God is love and he that dwells in love, dwells in God." (1 John 4:16)

Love, in this world's system, is influenced and limited by how people look, act, smell or dress. God is not affected by these things. He does not just have a form of pity and love for mankind. He IS love. (John 17)

A relationship with God must become so balanced and real that a person does not just have love, but must allow His perfect love to pour out of them and become a part of them.

Who Can Experience the Gifts of The Spirit?

Peter said the promise of the Holy Spirit is for **all** those who were there on the Day of Pentecost and to **all** that are called, and their children, and even those that are yet to come throughout history.

"For the promise is unto you, and to your children, and to all that are afar off, even as many as the Lord our God shall call."(Acts 2:39)

We were not living on the Day of Pentecost so we were not present when the Holy Spirit was first poured out 2,000 years ago. Our day of Pentecost is today. We do not have to wait in an upper room for the Holy Spirit to arrive. He's already here.

This promise is for all people and their children and even their descendants that are afar off yet and have not even been born. This will be available to everyone from now to the end of this age.

"Wherefore be ye not unwise, but understanding what the will of the Lord is. And be not drunk with wine, wherein is excess; but be filled with the Spirit; Speaking to yourselves in psalms and hymns and spiritual songs, singing and making melody in your heart to the Lord;" (Ephesians 5:17-19)

Being drunk with wine is the state of a person under the control of liquor. His manner will be unnatural and erratic because he has allowed himself to be controlled by something other than himself. Contrast this with a man under the control and influence of the Holy Spirit. He, too, will do things that are unnatural (they will be supernatural) but never erratic.

"Be filled" is not an option or a suggestion but is a direct command to believers. It should be a continuous experience; "keep on being filled with the Spirit" better conveys the meaning of this passage of scripture.

All believers should desire these spiritual gifts that are available.

Stir Up the Gifts of The Spirit

The gifts of God are not to receive and then set on a shelf and never use again. What a wasteful thought. Yet there are people who receive their new prayer language and after one session, never use it again. They mistakenly feel like they have experienced it and now it is of no further use to them. A constant flow of the Spirit is needed to refresh us. *"Stir up the gifts that are within you."* (2 Timothy 1:6)

We need to stir up those gifts that God has placed within us. Contrast this with a kettle of soup sitting on the stove. It needs to be stirred to keep the ingredients evenly distributed and seasoned. If it sits too long, all the real good stuff goes down to the bottom. Before serving, it needs stirring.

If believers periodically do not stir themselves up spiritually, all the godly truths, revelations, faith or joy that they have experienced can settle down and go dormant.

It is a fact that the gifts and calling of God are without repentance. In other words, God does not take back the gifts that He has given. But when they are not used for an extended period, we can feel like they are lost. They are not lost, they become dormant and they do need stirring up each day by spending time reading God's Word and in prayerful communication with God

Just as in a marriage relationship, the more time a person takes with their spouse communicating and spending intimate time together, the stronger their bond will become..

Do Not Neglect the Gifts

"Neglect not the gift that is in you, which was given you by prophecy with the laying on of hands of the presbytery." (1 Timothy 4:14)

The gifts should never become common place so they are treated carelessly. Give honor and glory to God when He chooses to use His gifts. All "spirit filled" Christians need a continual replenishing of the power of the Holy Spirit.

A person can be hospitalized and kept alive by using life-support systems, but they are barely existing. Christians can stay alive spiritually by barely existing, but they are not experiencing the abundant life that Christ offered. Every believer can benefit by a fresh infilling of the Holy Spirit in their life.

Strive to Abound in The Gifts.

"Strive to abound in the gifts." (1 Corinthians 14:12) God gives everyone permission to be spiritually motivated to excellence. Jesus has placed a high priority on His promises because He wants His people to experience His power on a regular basis.

"Some people have a difficult time understanding how to cultivate or develop a gift that is supernaturally empowered. This difficulty stems from viewing the miraculous gifts as magical or mechanical. We have no difficulty comprehending that a teacher can grow in the gift of teaching, or an evangelist in the gift of evangelism. So why is it difficult to believe that someone can grow in the gift of healing or prophecy?"(Charisma Magazine, p. 60, Sept. 1993).

"The truth is that we can grow in every spiritual exercise and every spiritual gift. Cultivating spiritual gifts requires attempting to use them on a regular basis."(Ibid, p. 63,64).

The United States of America realizes its crucial need of power in order to accomplish its goals and maintain peace. Jesus Christ knew His disciples needed the power of Pentecost. The last command that Jesus gave His disciples just before He ascended into heaven was for them to experience the power of Pentecost.

Do Not Be Ignorant of Spiritual Gifts.

This brings full circle the scripture in 1 Corinthians 12:1 where we are told not to be ignorant of spiritual gifts. That then, is what this study is all about. Believers are commanded to be workers in the Word, who are approved of God. Through the Word and the Holy Spirit all the spiritual equipment and provision needed have been provided. Discover the magnetism, the miracle, the mission, and the meaning of Pentecost.

THE GIFTS OF THE HOLY SPIRIT ARE FOR YOU!

Gifts in the Old Testament

In the Old Testament the Holy Spirit came upon certain men and women to empower them for a short season to do a certain work. A few examples of these people would include the following:

Joseph *"And Pharaoh said unto his servants, Can we find such a one as this is, a man in whom the spirit of God is?"* (Genesis 41:38)

Moses *"And I will come down and talk with thee there: and I will take of the spirit which is upon thee, and will put it upon them; and they shall bear the burden of the people with thee, that thou bear it not thyself alone."* (Numbers 11:17)

Joshua *"And Joshua the son of Nun was full of the spirit of wisdom; for Moses has laid his hands upon him: and the children of Israel harkened unto him and did as the Lord commanded Moses. And the Lord said unto Moses, Take thee Joshua the son of Nun, a man in whom is the spirit, and lay thine hand upon him;"* (Deuteronomy 34:9 & Numbers 27:18)

David *"The spirit of the Lord spake by me, and his word was in my tongue."* (II Samuel 23:2)

Elisha *"And it came to pass, when they were gone over, that Elijah said unto Elisha, Ask what I shall do for thee, before I be taken away from thee. And Elisha said, I pray thee, let a double portion of thy spirit be upon me. And when the sons of the prophets which were to view at Jericho saw him, they said, The spirit of Elijah doth rest on Elisha. and they came to meet him, and bowed themselves to the ground before him"* (II Kings 2:9,15)

Daniel *"But at the last Daniel came in before me, whose name was Belteshazzar, according to the name of my god, and in whom is the spirit of the holy gods: and before him I told the dream, saying, . . . There is a man in thy kingdom, in whom is the spirit of the holy gods; and in the days of thy father light and understanding and wisdom, like the wisdom of the gods, was found in him; Then this Daniel was preferred above the presidents and princes, because an excellent spirit was in him; and the king thought to set him over the whole realm."* (Daniel 4:8, 5:11, 6:3)

Micah *"But truly I am full of power by the spirit of the Lord, and of judgment, and of might, to declare unto Jacob his transgres-*

sion, and to Israel his sin." (Micah 3:8)

Only since Christ's death and resurrection can mankind now have the opportunity for the Holy spirit to come and live inside of him permanently. Believers may now experience the ongoing power and presence of the Holy Spirit, which has been given to help them in every avenue of life. Christians today critically need all that Christ provided for the first century Church, therefore we must not come behind in any of the gifts or callings of God.

THE GIFTS OF THE HOLY SPIRIT ARE FOR YOU!

CHAPTER 4

SYMBOLS OF THE HOLY SPIRIT

The Bible uses various symbols to describe the Holy Spirit in both the Old and New Testaments. To more fully understand the person and work of the Holy Spirit it is well to have an overview of the different symbols.

A Dove

Perhaps the most recognized symbol of the Holy Spirit is that of a dove. The dove is typical of gentleness (Matt. 10:16), sacrifice (Gen. 15:9), purity (Lev. 12:6,8; Luke 2:24), a special anointing (Num.6:10), and harmlessness (Matthew 10:16).

The dove, being ceremonially clean, was used as a trespass offering for sin under the Old Covenant (Lev. 5:7-10; 12:8).

A dove was symbolic of the Holy Spirit as He descended on Jesus, denoting Him as our sin offering, at His water baptism in Matt. 3:16; Mark 1:9-11; Luke 3:22 and John 1:32. In each of these passages the dove is described as representing the Holy Spirit specifically.

The first mention of the Holy Spirit in scripture shows Him acting in a bird-like fashion. *"The Spirit of God was [hovering, brooding] over the face of the waters."* (Genesis 1:2 Amplified Bible)

"In His relationships to men, the Spirit as a dove primarily works by gently leading and persuasions, and He seldom demands or compels. As the heavenly dove indwelling the believer's heart, He delights in conveying the peace of God and in proclaiming the fact of peace with God. He is most pleased when the heart in which He abides maintains those qualities of gracious godliness that best reflects His own nature." (Holdcroft. 1979. pp. 31-32.)

We also see the Holy Spirit symbolically being presented in the New Testament first as a dove.

"Just as the dove is a universal symbol of peace, so the Holy Spirit is also God's agent to bring peace to the human heart. This is a very fitting simile for the blessed Holy Spirit." (Riggs. 1977. p. 78.)

OIL

Oil is symbolic of the Holy Spirit's anointing, a widely used symbol. In the Old Testament there were special oils mixed for sacrificial duties, the anointing of priests and the anointing of kings. No one dared use this oil for any other purpose than what it was intended. There were to be no counterfeits made and no common oil could be used for these ceremonies. (Exodus 30:32) Any attempt to substitute the anointing oil would remove God's anointing and it would only be an effort of the flesh at work.

"This anointing represented a separation and sanctification of the person unto a holy purpose. It also represented the divine enablement and qualification for that ministry. No one dared enter one of these particular ministries without it." (Iverson. 1976. p.9)

"As Jesus, the great antitype of prophet, priest and king, stood up to preach in Nazareth, He said, *'The Spirit of the Lord is upon me, because He hath anointed me' (Luke 4:18)*. The anointing which came upon our Great Head was *'like the precious ointment upon the head, that ran down upon the beard, even Aaron's beard: that went down to the skirts of his garments.' (Psalm 133:2)* The anointing which came on Christ flows down to the remotest member of His body who will accept the precious ointment." (Riggs. 1978. p.72.)

Each person as they begin their walk with Christ is anointed with a special anointing by God Himself. Each one is selected for special duty and privilege under the anointing that flows down the entire body of Christ. *we are a part of the "whole"*

"It is mentioned frequently in the Old Testament as a pre-figure of the fullness of the Spirit in the believer. Oil was included in the meal offerings presented to the Lord (Lev. 22) and was the fuel for the

1 Cor. 1:21

Give me oil in my lamp —
Light of World — Matt 5:14-16

lamp in the Holy Place." (Exodus 27:20) (Jepson. 1975. p.27)

The disciples anointed the sick with oil and they were healed in Mark 6:13. Present day believers are instructed to do the same when praying for the sick in James 5:14.

Jesus mentioned the virgins whose lamps ran out of oil while they were waiting for the bridegroom in Matthew 25:1-13. Believers are urged to be full of the Spirit always. There was a special oil that kept the lamp burning inside the Holy Place (Exodus 27:20). This oil was typical of the Holy Spirit in a person's life . . . continuously burning and flowing.

The oil is a picture of the Holy Spirit's total involvement in the daily life of each believer.

"Oil penetrates, permeates and saturates. It soothes, moistens and protects. It lubricates, eliminating friction and abrasion. It purges and cleanses. Its energy radiates light and warmth. And edible oils have nutritional value." (Jepson. 1975. p.28.).

WATER

Jesus told the Samaritan woman at the well that water was symbolic of the Holy Spirit indwelling the believer at the new birth. *"But whosoever drinketh of the water that I shall give him shall never thirst; but the water that I shall give him shall be in him a well of water springing up into everlasting life."(John 4:14)* This water of life is drawn up with joy from the well of salvation (Isaiah 12:3).

Water has many uses, it cleanses, washes away filth, purifies, satisfies thirst, refreshes, sustains life and causes growth. Plants, animals and mankind could not survive without water. Without the Holy Spirit we are not able to sustain a spiritual life reconciled to Christ.

Just as the ground gets parched without water, our spiritual life becomes dead and parched without the renewing of the Holy Spirit. Jesus said he came to give us abundant life and yet how sad it is to see people famishing for lack of spiritual water when all they need to do is draw water from the River of Life. The Psalmist says that we should be like trees planted by the rivers of water (Psalm 1:3). He also mentioned that because of our planting, we shall flourish.

Paul said Christ wanted to sanctify and cleanse the Church with the washing of water by the Word. (Ephesians 5:26) He wants His Church holy and pure. The way He has arranged for us to acquire that state is by the Holy Spirit washing us continuously with the Word of God and Christ continuously cleansing us from all unrighteousness (1 John 1:7).

Water became symbolic of the Holy Spirit in Jesus' prophecy of the outpouring of the Holy Spirit in John 7:38-39. *"He that believeth on Me, as the Scripture hath said, out of his belly shall flow rivers of living water. (But this spake he of the Spirit, which they that believe on Him should receive: for the Holy Ghost was not yet given; because that Jesus was not yet glorified)."*

This water gushes forth from the very innermost being of the believer, it symbolizes the Holy Spirit baptism that inundates the total person in the things of the Spirit. Paul refers to the coming of the Holy Spirit as being "poured out" upon all flesh (Acts 2:17,18). These examples are not of a stagnant pool, but of a torrent of power surging or gushing forth.

WIND AND BREATH

The wind symbolizes the mysterious unseen work of the Holy Spirit.

"The wind bloweth where it listeth, and thou hearest the sound thereof, but canst not tell whence it cometh, and whither it goeth; so is every one that is born of the Spirit" (John 3:8). *"And suddenly there came a sound from heaven as of a rushing mighty wind, and it filled all the house where they were sitting. And there appeared unto them cloven tongues like as fire, and it sat upon each of them (Acts 2:2-3).*

The Holy Spirit, like the wind, is strong and unrestrained in its movements, persistent, pervading and refreshing.

The dry bones of Ezekiel were brought back to life by the Holy Spirit blowing like a wind to revive them. The Holy Spirit wants to revive all the spiritual dry bones. Believers need to listen for the winds of the Spirit when they begin to blow.

"So I prophesied as I was commanded: as I prophesied, there was a noise, and behold a shaking, and the bones came together, bone to his bone. And when I beheld, lo, the sinews, and the flesh came up

upon them, and the skin covered them above: but there was no breath in them. Then said He unto me, Prophesy unto the wind, thus said the Lord God; Come from the four winds, O Breath, and breathe upon these slain, that they may live. So I prophesied as He commanded me, and the breath came into them, and they lived, and stood upon these slain, that they may live." (Ezekiel 37:7-10).

"The fact that the usual Hebrew and Greek terms for Spirit (*ruach, pneuma*) each translates not only 'spirit' but also 'breath' or 'wind' further supports the symbolism. The Holy Spirit is designated as the out-breathing of God, so that He constitutes the atmosphere within which the believer lives." (Holdcroft, 1979. p. 28)

"The wind goeth toward the south, and turneth about unto the north; it whirleth continually, and the wind returneth again according to the circuits ."(Ecclesiastes 1:6

The Holy Spirit has a special circuit of service in relation to the redeemed . . . He encloses us in His love, encircles us in His presence, encompasses us about with His power, and environs us through His Word. (Marsh. 1963. p.219.)

A SEAL

A special Holy Spirit seal is placed upon each believer, showing that they belong to Christ.

"In whom ye also trusted, after that ye heard the word of truth, the gospel of your salvation: in whom also, after that ye believed, ye were sealed with that Holy Spirit of promise ."(Ephesians 1:13)

"Who hath also sealed us, and given the earnest of the Spirit in our hearts." (II Corinthians 1:22)

Three times scripture states that the Holy Spirit is the earnest of our inheritance (II Corinthians 5:5; Ephesians 1:14 and Ephesians 4:30).

According to the dictionary, the meaning of earnest is: Earnest money, a pledge, something that stands for part of the price and paid beforehand to confirm the transaction. Used in the New Testament only in a figurative sense and spoken of the Holy Spirit which God has given to believers in this present life to assure them of their future and eternal inheritance. Firstfruits, a deposit (Zodhiates. 1993. p. 257 No. 728.).

THE GIFTS OF THE HOLY SPIRIT ARE FOR YOU!

He has given us the Holy Spirit in Pentecostal fullness, not only in the initial infilling according to Acts 2:4 but also in the privilege of a Spirit-filled life. Paul calls this an earnest or first installment. This is more than a foretaste. It is an actual participation in what will be ours in all its fullness in the life to come. In Romans 8:23 Paul calls it the firstfruits of the Spirit. The firstfruits were always an actual part of the harvest. Thus, the Spirit is given to us as a real part of, and a present experience of our future inheritance.

We read also that "if the Spirit of him that raised up Jesus from the dead dwell [continues to live] in you, he that raised up Christ from the dead shall also quicken [resurrect] your mortal bodies by his Spirit that dwelleth in you." (Romans 8:11)

"Then John makes it even more practical as he says, 'Every man that hath this hope in him purifieth himself, even as he is pure'" (1 John 3:3) (Adult Teacher. 1978. p.318).

This is a reference to the Old Testament practice of receiving a very small portion of that which has been purchased or promised as a token and pledge that the full purchase will be delivered in due time. By this means it is indicated to us that this glorious experience, which we usually call the Baptism in the Holy Spirit, is but a sample and a foretaste of that effulgence of glory which will be ours at the coming of our Lord.(Riggs. 1977. p.75).

"And grieve not the holy Spirit of God, whereby ye are sealed unto the day of redemption." (Ephesians 4:30).

The seal of the Holy Spirit hides us in Christ who is hid in God. The only way the seal can be broken is if we purposely grieve the Holy Spirit and turn away from the things of God. When the seal is broken, the impurities get in and we are no longer preserved blamelessly.

"Nevertheless the foundation of God standeth sure, having this seal, The Lord knoweth them that are his. And, Let every one that nameth the name of Christ depart from iniquity." (II Timothy 2:19)

**"I will teach thee and instruct thee
in the way which thou shalt go."
Psalm 32:8**

Diagram 5.1

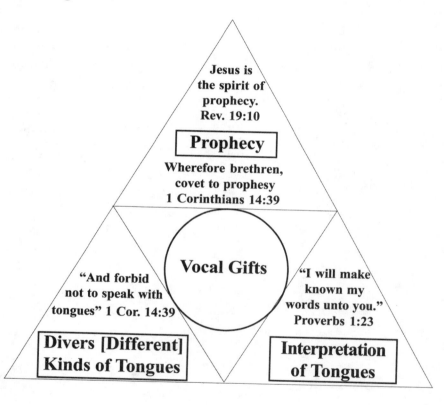

**We are to desire spiritual gifts. I Corinthians 14:1
He will give you the desire of your heart. Psalm 37:4**

CHAPTER 5

THE GIFT OF TONGUES

"For with stammering lips and another tongue will He speak to this people, with whom He said this is the rest wherewith I will cause the weary to rest and this is the refreshing, yet they would not hear." (Isaiah 28:11,12)

Paul quoted this Old Testament passage in I Corinthians 14:21, indicating it fulfilled prophecy with the coming of the gifts of different kinds of tongues. According to Paul, the tongues given by the Holy Spirit not only make intercession, but will build up and cause a person to be refreshed in spirit, soul and body.

Practioneers of hypnosis or a passive mind state promise relaxation and spiritual revelation, but it is evident from the weight of scripture that they are just sorry counterfeits of God's genuine gifts of the Spirit.

Speaking in tongues is manifest in two distinct ways. Whenever a tongue given during a worship service is distinctly heard above the rest of the congregation it is the gift of tongues and it should be followed by an interpretation in the known language. (I Corinthians 14:27) This kind of message is given by God to build up the Church. In an individual's prayer life, a tongue spoken to God in worship edifies [builds up] the believer and makes intercession for his needs, and those of others. (1 Corinthians 14:2) *Romans 8:26.*

Private Devotional Tongues

The most widely accepted doorway experience that unlocks the active working of all the gifts of the Spirit is called the Baptism of the Holy Spirit with the accompanying manifestation of speaking in a new prayer language. These languages become private devotional tongues that are used to make intercession, give praise to God and edify the person.

Natural prayers are often dominated by egotistical demands on God, fears and even doubts. Believers get into prayer habits of telling God how, when and where to answer their prayers. Jesus instructed the believers in John 14,15 and 16 to just *ask* the Father in His name and it would be done.

The Holy Spirit guides prayers into a perfect approach to the throne of God and makes direct intercession from His observation of all the details. We must learn to trust the intercession that the Holy Spirit makes for them. *Roms 8: 26*

Without this initial experience of tongues that accompanies the Baptism of the Holy Spirit, the nine gifts of the Holy Spirit may appear from time to time, but as a rule will not be consistently present. People can live on the fringes for many years and yet not enjoy the total benefits of what the Holy Spirit has for them.

⋆ It was prophesied that Jesus would baptize with the Holy Ghost and fire. Therefore, the terminology of Holy Ghost or Holy Spirit Baptism is correct usage. On the Day of Pentecost, Jesus fulfilled the prophecy and sent the Holy Spirit baptizing the believers who were gathered awaiting the Promise given to them. The Promise came with the sound of a mighty rushing wind and fire, ushering in a new era of believers who spoke as the Holy Spirit gave them the utterance or vocabulary. This new advent had been prophesied in Joel 2:28,29 and Isaiah 28:11 and fulfilled at Pentecost.

"And when the day of Pentecost was fully come, they were all with one accord in one place. And suddenly there came a sound from heaven as of a rushing mighty wind, and it filled all the house where they were sitting. And there appeared unto them cloven tongues like as of fire, and it sat upon each of them. And they were all filled with the Holy Ghost, and began to speak with other tongues, as the Spirit gave them utterance." (Acts 2:1-4)

You will note here, the believers did the speaking [made vocal sounds] as the Holy Spirit gave them the expression or vocabulary.

Devotional tongues can be initiated or stopped any time or place by the believer, just as he initiates prayer in his own known language. Tongues are an outward sign that during prayer time a person has learned to surrender an unruly tongue to the Holy Spirit. At the time of surrender, the fullness of the Holy Spirit is released into a person's spirit and has a renewing effect on the spirit, soul and body. This does not mean from that moment on a person will be perfect and never walk in the flesh again, it just means they have learned to yield control of their life to the Holy Spirit. Each person is responsible after that to discipline themselves to be consistent with their dedication.

"But you, beloved, build yourselves up [founded] on your most holy faith—make progress, rise like an edifice higher and higher—praying in the Holy Spirit." (Jude 20 The Amplified Bible)

"Praying in the Spirit enables you to pray the perfect will of God. It allows you to step out of the realm of the flesh and into the realm of the Spirit so that no matter how weak or ignorant you may be in the natural, you can pray exactly as you need to." (Copeland. Sept. 1992. p. 12) Roms 8:26.

This infilling of the Holy Spirit with the accompaniment of a personal prayer language was an accepted experience by some great leaders of the Church. Finney, Murrey, Miller, Myer, Moule, A.J. Gordon, Wesley, Moody, Chapman, A. B. Simpson and many others all believed this was a distinct experience beyond that of salvation.

How Can A Person Receive
Their Personal Prayer Language?

Every born-again believer, at one time or another, comes to a personal crisis in their prayer and worship. They discover they cannot express their deepest desires to God properly in their native language. Their desires exceed their natural abilities as they hunger for a mode of superior communication about the spiritual matters at hand.

The first step in receiving the fullness of the Spirit is to ask for it.

"If ye then, being evil, know how to give good gifts unto your children: how much more shall your heavenly Father give the Holy Spirit to them that ask him?" (Luke 11:13) Next, according to the prophecy of Isaiah 28:11,12, quoted earlier, the starting point begins

with a stammering lip and proceeds to another tongue. Two half-steps are all that are required to enter this new full-tide of blessing. A person begins by making stammering sounds. Any combination of sounds may be chosen while lifting them up in worship to the Lord. There are hundreds of vocal combinations, but as a person begins to speak, the Holy Spirit immediately honors the faith of the person involved and begins to birth a fluency and vocabulary in these sounds.

The sounds do not need to be deciphered or understood by the natural mind. They are coming out of the mind of the Holy Spirit. The believer's part is to continue making the audible sounds. It is impossible to speak a language without making sounds. It is the Holy Spirit's part to help change the sounds that we initiate effortlessly, from one new sound to another, until there is a fluency of worship to the Lord. These sounds can be sung or spoken. Within moments of starting, a person will notice that the sounds begin to flow out of their innermost being like the rivers of living water Jesus prophesied about in John 7:37-38. The only personal thought needed is when to begin and when to stop, which will always be controlled by the individual doing the praying. Total focus of attention should always be on praise, worship and adoration to the Lord.

After the initial reception of a prayer language, the more often a person uses their new language, the more proficient they will become. Fluency depends on how much a person allows the Holy Spirit to create new variations of sounds. The vocabulary of the Holy Spirit is only hindered by the limitations the believer puts on Him.

"Speaking in tongues—or any other spiritual gift—is not unbiblical or outmoded, not a status symbol or a substitute for spiritual growth. Above all, spiritual language is not divisive. When the beauty of this exercise is scripturally understood and wisely employed, it is a pathway of blessing for the entire body of Christ." (Hayford. Mar. 1993.)

Can Satan Understand Tongues?

Can Satan understand tongues? This has been a question that has been widely discussed. People often take the stand that Satan does not have the ability to understand a prayer language. Scripture, on the other hand, demonstrates an interesting paradox concerning

Job 29.21-22
James 5:7
Hosea 6:3
Zach 10:1

this issue.

Notice, that when a person speaks in tongues he is speaking in the languages of men and of angels according to Paul. *"Though I speak with the tongues of men and of angels..."* I Corinthians 13:1)

The question then becomes, does Satan understand all the languages that have ever been spoken on the earth? The evident answer is an emphatic, yes. He has been fluent and involved in knowing all the various languages and dialects of the earth even from the beginning. He has used every language to tempt people throughout the ages. Jesus said in Matthew 16:23 that Satan's understanding is very developed in the areas concerning mankind.

Secondly, Satan can also understand the language of the angelic beings. He was created as Lucifer the covering cherub of heaven before he conceived sin in his mind and was cast out. Satan still accuses people day and night in heaven before God. (Job 1:6-12; Revelation 12:10) Isa.

An assumption can be made that if Satan understands all the languages of earth, present and past plus the angelic language then he can also understand a prayer language composed of those spoken by, *"men or of angels."*

Here is where the Word of God shows us a fragment of God's great storehouse of wisdom. Paul clarifies what takes place when someone speaks in a prayer language:

"For he that speaketh in an unknown tongue speaketh not unto men, but unto God: for no man understandeth him; howbeit in the spirit he speaketh mysteries." (I Corinthians 14:2)

When a person speaks to God in their prayer language, *spiritual mysteries* are spoken. In other words, Satan may understand the words spoken, but he does not understand the meaning. It's like a coded message using common, everyday words but Satan does not have a decoder and will never break the code. Only God knows what the Spirit is saying through a person when they are praying in their heavenly language.

Satan has had a problem understanding spiritual things for many years.

"Howbeit we speak wisdom among them that are perfect: yet not the wisdom of this world, nor of the princes of this world, that

41

come to nought: But we speak the wisdom of God in a mystery, even the hidden wisdom, which God ordained before the world unto our glory: Which none of the princes of this world knew: for had they known it, they would not have crucified the Lord of glory." (I Corinthians 2:6-8).

The fact that Satan does not understand spiritual truths becomes evident from the fact that Jesus openly declared his mission often, even prophesying his manner of death and resurrection that would secure redemption for all mankind.

"I am the living bread which came down from heaven: if any man eat of this bread, he shall live for ever: and the bread that I will give is my flesh, which I will give for the life of the world (John 6:51).

If Satan had understood, he would never have allowed anyone to kill Jesus, and thus overturned God's eternal plan of salvation for mankind.

Many people refer to a person's prayer language as a "hot line to heaven," and indeed it is. It is one of the most powerful weapons a Christian can have in his spiritual arsenal. Satan has tried to discourage believers from receiving this language through the years because it leaves him without any game plan to use against them when they are praying in the Spirit. He has no idea how the Holy Spirit is making intercession for their needs.

"The devil has tried to hide the simplicity of it from us because he knows if we ever start doing it, he will have no place left. The truth is, he is limited. He cannot touch your reborn spirit. The only thing he has to work on is your flesh. Once you learn what brings the flesh under dominion, once you learn that praying in the Spirit applies spirit to flesh and causes the flesh to obey God the way it ought to, the devil won't be able to get a foothold in your life at all!" (Hayford. March 1993.)

Different Kinds of Tongues-Congregational

The Gift of Divers [different] Kinds of Tongues (from now on called the gift of tongues), was given to the Church to edify the Body of Christ in public meetings. The congregational gift of tongues referred to herein cannot be initiated any time at the will of a person as in the use of the personal prayer language; it is initiated and given when the Holy Spirit wills for it to be used. To be properly used it must also be accompanied by the Gift of Interpretation of Tongues so the whole group or congregation can understand the Holy Spirit's message.

Not everyone will be used by the Spirit to give a message in public. The Holy Spirit does the choosing about whom He will use to deliver a gift. He will never force a person to do anything against his will or contrary to his own personality. The Holy Spirit responds to the willingness of each individual and then stirs them, or bears witness in their spirit that He would like to use them. If an individual is willing to set aside his own timidity and rely on the leading of the Holy Spirit, he can speak the sounds, words or phrases given to him so they can be interpreted into the language of the listeners.

During the interim of waiting for an interpretation of tongues, all the people present should be in an attitude of prayer and expectation to hear what it is the Holy Spirit wants to say. Individuals who want to be used of the Holy Spirit for the interpretation should be waiting with a quietness in their spirit to hear the voice of the Spirit as He wants to use them to either speak out the meaning of the message or to confirm what has been spoken by another person.

The gift of tongues is designed for the edification of the Church. Paul prohibits the use of the gift of tongues if there is no one present who will give the interpretation of tongues. "*But if there be no interpreter, let him keep silence in the church; and let him speak to himself, and to God* (I Corinthians 14:28)."

Paul also presents another possibility for the interpretation of tongues. "

*Wherefore let him that speaketh in an unknown tongue pray that he may interpret (*I Corinthians 14:13)."

The one who has the faith to speak the message in tongues can exercise the same faith to believe God for the interpretation. However, if a message is given and not interpreted by anyone, including himself, he is not to give a second message during that meeting.

Edification is always the most effective test of whether a gift has been used properly.

"How is it then, brethren? when ye come together, every one of you hath a psalm, hath a doctrine, hath a tongue, hath a revelation,

hath an interpretation. Let all things be done unto edifying." (1 Cor. 14:26)

"Let all things be done decently and in order (1 Corinthians 14:40).*"*

People new to the gifts, or ignorant of this verse, often are tempted to speak out under the anointing without waiting for the proper timing. When the unction of the Spirit is on a person, it is the responsibility of that person to patiently await God for His exact instructions about when to give the message. The principle here is the same that controls the vocal gift of prophecy. *"And the spirits of the prophets are subject to the prophets* (1 Cor. 14:32).*"*

Each person has the ability to speak or remain silent. Each individual also has the responsibility to restrain from speaking or to speak with authority when the time allows, but the Holy Spirit will never force anyone to do anything against His timing or their will.

An evil spirit, in contrast, tries to push aside the human personality and take over by force in order to interrupt what the Holy Spirit is doing at the moment. Satan sometimes even tries to use counterfeit tongues to cause confusion among newer believers.

The messages in tongues that are genuine will bring a reassurance and witness in the spirits of the listeners. A sense of God's presence is increased and a person's spirit should be strengthened by a message in tongues followed by the interpretation.

When a person receives a message in tongues, he speaks until the unction of the Spirit stops giving words. When the words from the Holy Spirit stop, so should the person giving the message. Anything added from that point on would be a work of the flesh.

The gift of tongues must be accompanied by the Gift of Interpretation of Tongues. The two of these together are equal to the singular Gift of Prophecy. It's like the sum of two nickels equal a dime. Neither the gift of tongues nor the gift of interpretation alone equal the gift of prophecy. Together these twins equal prophecy, and as a result should bless the whole group or Church.

Paul set a limit of three messages on tongues that were to be spoken in any one service in I Corinthians 14:27 and he insisted on the interpretation of the messages. It is also possible to have three prophetic messages in a service. After making these rules, in verse

39, he instructed that tongues are not to be forbidden in the congregation. Paul recognized the benefit of God being able to use this method as a sign to the unbeliever. God uses common, ordinary people to give messages with the immediate revelation of its meaning through the gift of interpretation of tongues.

There must always be balance to the use of the various gifts during the meeting of believers so that there is also adequate time for exhortation and preaching from the Word of God along with worship to the Lord. When imbalance occurs, confusion also occurs and Paul said, "*For God is not the author of confusion, but of peace, as in all the churches of the saints. (1 Cor. 14:35)*"

How to Give a Message in Tongues

The best way to be ready to give a message in tongues is to practice using a private prayer language on a regular basis. Then when the unction of the Holy Spirit begins to stir a person's spirit during a meeting, they can respond to the Holy Spirit's quickening because they have fine-tuned themselves to the anointing.

The next step is to wait for the right timing. A message in tongues or its interpretation is never used to interrupt another speaker or the preaching of God's Word.

When the right time presents itself, the person should speak loud enough to be heard, using a clear, pleasing voice that does not distract from the message they are delivering. When God stops the flow of anointed words, the speaker stops speaking.

The first speaker should then quietly thank God and await the interpretation. If there is no interpretation, he or she should pray that God will give it to him or her. Remember, if He gave the anointing for the original message in tongues, He can also give the interpretation. A person should be as willing to do one, as well as the other, or both, if necessary, to maintain the proper order.

THE GIFTS OF THE HOLY SPIRIT ARE FOR YOU!

CHAPTER 6

INTERPRETATION OF
TONGUES

God Himself ordained that there should be a Gift of Tongues otherwise there would not be any reason for Him to have given the complimentary Gift of Interpretation of Tongues to make the message known. The gift of different kinds of tongues often is a forerunner to get people ready to listen to what God is going to say through the interpretation of those tongues. After the message in tongues has been delivered, people should be in an attitude of listening and prayer. Then when the interpretation of tongues is given by the Holy Spirit it should be readily received into the hearts of the listeners. *"I will make known my words to you"* (Proverbs 1:23). *"I will teach thee and instruct thee in the way which thou shalt go"* (Psalm 32:8).

The Holy Spirit applies and quickens His message to the people He specifically wants to communicate with by bearing witness in their spirit when they hear the words of the interpretation. *"For as many as are led by the Spirit of God, they are the sons of God. The Spirit itself beareth witness with our spirit, that we are the children of God:"* (Romans 8:14,16).

People should not try to apply the interpretation to one another as that is a work of the flesh trying to manipulate circumstances. The Holy Spirit is perfectly capable of confirming or bearing witness in a person's heart all by Himself without the aid of well-meaning, but sometimes misguided bystanders.

After a message in tongues is given the Holy Spirit looks for people willing to speak His words of edification, exhortation, comfort, or on occasion, correction.

God begins by giving an unction or quickening in the spirit of the person He chooses. They start to receive words, phrases or whole ideas in their spirit that immediately move into their mind. Then they begin to frame them in their own words and express the thought God has given to them.

The words of the interpretation should be spoken in the normal language the person uses. God is not confined to, nor impressed with, a particular style, such as old King James English. He is interested in getting the message to His people.

People delivering an audible message from God should not shriek or detract from the message by allowing emotions or body movements to dominate the situation. The person speaks until the message has been clearly given and then stops. The vessel the Holy Spirit uses should not add to the message or embellish it in any way.

Paul's desire was, *"Wherefore, brethren, covet to prophesy and forbid not to speak with tongues. Let all things be done decently and in order."* (I Corinthians 14:39,40)

The process of giving an interpretation to a tongue is much the same as when a person receives a Word of Knowledge or a Word of Prophecy, etc. God gives a person the words or thoughts and they proceed to speak them out by faith. The message should be spoken clearly in a pleasing natural voice that can be heard by all. As a person becomes more comfortable speaking or doing something under the anointing of the Holy Spirit, God uses them more often in the gift areas.

All the words that are spoken must agree with written scripture. If there is any question, the message is always open to judgment by others who are seasoned in the Word of God and also walk in the gifts of the Spirit.

Does the Interpreter Understand the Tongue?

A person who is interpreting the gift of tongues hardly ever understands the message with his own mind. It is a supernatural gift of interpretation. It is not a translation. The Holy Spirit is the one who is giving the vocabulary or thoughts to be spoken. Consequently sometimes the message in tongues can take quite a space of time and the interpretation will be very short or the message in tongues short and the interpretation long. The human element at this point enters the picture. It takes some people longer to say something, whereas others may use only a few words to get the same idea across.

Can The Interpretation Ever Be A Literal Translation?

There may be occasions when a listener is knowledgeable of various languages and hears one known by him. He can give a literal translation of what he hears. The Holy Spirit is free to choose how He will do things. There have been many instances recorded where a listener heard and understood perfectly what the Holy Spirit spoke through other people.

As a missionary for twenty years, I heard this happen on various occasions in meetings where people were receiving their prayer language. They would speak phrases in English or Latin. Both languages were understood by my natural mind. The people were glorifying God in languages they had never learned, and did not understand, as they received their new prayer languages.

Paul says in 1 Corinthians 13:1, that it may be with the "tongues of men or of angels" that we speak. We may know some languages of the earth, but we do not know all of them past, nor present. We do not know the language of angels apart from the gift of the Holy Spirit.

The Tower of Babel, built by Nimrod, in the land of Shinar was to magnify man's pride and bring continual unity through their knowledge of a common language. God dispersed the people and confused their languages so no one understood the other.

It is interesting to note that God said in Genesis 11:6, *"Behold, the people is one, and they have all one language; and this they begin to do: and now nothing will be restrained from them, which they have imagined to do."* God kept them from doing what they had imagined they could do.

Pentecost reversed the curse of Babel and gave God's people a common heavenly language that can once again be understood by all as it is communicated to each listener by the Holy Spirit. This language is not to magnify man, but God. It is to bring unity in the

Spirit, not disunity. It is the very means by which God can enable mankind to do whatever is in His plan to reach planet earth with the gospel before Jesus returns for His Church.

Satan's world system is still desperately trying to set up a communications network that will link the whole world with its more than 6,700 separate languages together again with one voice. Satan is trying to counterfeit what the Holy Spirit has already accomplished. The World Wide Web is using everything from computers and modems to esoteric experiences in their vain attempt to unite people and their thinking globally. Their quantum leaps of technology are just weak counterfeits in comparison to God's great design.

Only believers are enabled to speak a common heavenly language with the potential of accomplishing great and mighty things. As people humble themselves to receive, God lifts them up and grants their heart's desire.

Can There Be More Than One Interpretation?

Each message should receive only one interpretation. Sometimes another person will follow with a word from the Lord. This is usually a word of prophecy, not a second interpretation. Even if others have the mind of the Lord for the interpretation, they are to allow the one who starts first to give the message. The bystanders can use the witness they have received to confirm the message. There should not be any competition. I Corinthians 14:27 says, *"If any man speak in an unknown tongue, let it be by two or at the most by three, and that by course; and let one interpret."*

Men and women are tools of the Holy Spirit, but they are also rational, free, cooperating partners, and therefore they are also responsible for maintaining order and edify the listeners.

Isa 63:10 - Grieving the Spirit -
Acts 5:1-5 - Vexed the Holy Spirit
Acts 1:51 - Resist " " "
Heb 10:29 - Rebel - "Insulted"
50 / Thess. 19.

CHAPTER 7

THE GIFT OF PROPHECY

The responsibility of the one giving prophecy is great because they become the mouthpiece of God to His people. The Hebrew word (Ro 'eh, used 309 times in the Old Testament) for 'to prophecy' means, *to put forth words abundantly from God's mind and by God's Spirit.* The Greek term 'prophetes' means, *to flow forth, be fluent, or to speak for another (*Stamps, 1992, p.1002). When the Holy Spirit speaks, the prophetic words should be spoken so everyone listening can understand the message.

"We know in part, and we prophesy in part . . . " (I Corinthians 13:8). Prophecy gives a small insight into God's Will for our lives.

"I will make known my words to you" (Proverbs 1:23). God is not trying to hide His mysteries from the Body of Christ, on the contrary, He wants to share them. He makes His mysteries known by the revelation of the Holy Spirit.

"But God hath revealed them unto us by his spirit: for the Spirit searcheth all things, yea, the deep things of God. For what man knoweth the things of a man save the spirit of man which is in him? even so the things of God knoweth no man, but the Spirit of God. Now we have received not the spirit of the world, but the spirit which is of God; that we might know the things that are freely given to us of God. Which things also we speak, not in the words which man's wisdom teacheth, but which the Holy Ghost teacheth: comparing spiritual things with spiritual" (I Corinthians 2:10-13).

THE GIFTS OF THE HOLY SPIRIT ARE FOR YOU!

The gift of prophecy is considered by many as the most important among the three vocal gifts because of Paul's exhortation to the Corinthian church. *"I would that ye all spake with tongues, but rather that ye prophesied: for greater is he that prophesieth than he that speaketh with tongues, except he interpret, that the church may receive edifying"* (I Corinthians 14:5).

When God uses prophecy to speak to His people, He speaks to them through a person who will deliver His message as the Holy Spirit guides him. As with the previous vocal gifts, God will not force anyone to speak who does not want to speak for Him. He looks for willing vessels who are willing to be heard. *"I heard the voice of the Lord, saying, Whom shall I send, and who will go for us? Then said I, Here am I; send me. And he said, Go, and tell this people, Hear ye indeed, but understand not; and see ye indeed, but perceive not"* (Isaiah 6:8,9).

Aaron became the spokesman or prophet of Moses. God wanted it this way to show the relationship of the prophet to God. *"And thou shalt speak unto him, and put words in his mouth: and I will be with thy mouth, and with his mouth, and will teach you what ye shall do. And he shall be to thee instead of a mouth, and thou shalt be to him instead of God"* (Exodus 4:15,16). *"And the LORD said unto Moses, See, I have made thee a god to Pharaoh: and Aaron thy brother shall be thy prophet"* (Exodus 7:1).

The obligation of the speaker is to speak the prophecy as God gives it. Then it is up to the Holy Spirit to apply it and the listeners to receive it.

"Moreover he said unto me, Son of man, all my words that I shall speak unto thee receive in thine heart, and hear with thine ears. And go, get thee to them of the captivity, unto the children of thy people, and speak unto them, and tell them, Thus saith the Lord GOD; whether they will hear, or whether they will forbear" (Ezekiel 10,11).

Looking at this, it is plain to see not all prophecies are going to be accepted by the listeners with open hearts. Some Old Testament prophets share how God told them to speak the word of prophecy. *"But the LORD said unto me, Say not, I am a child for thou shalt go to all that I shall send thee, and whatsoever I command thee thus shalt speak"* (Jeremiah 1:7).

52

Jeremiah was obedient to speak the word of God, even to the point of being put into a mud pit for the messages. Today the weight of reaction is on the listener once the message has been relayed to them. Some will hear and obey, while others will ignore the word of God and continue as if nothing had ever been spoken to them but God holds them accountable.

Numbers 12:6-8 records three ways of divine communication with prophets. *"If there be a prophet among you, I the Lord will make myself known unto him in a vision, and will speak unto him in a dream. My servant Moses is not so, who is faithful in all mine house. With him will I speak mouth to mouth, even apparently, and not in dark speeches."*

Another reason for acting responsibly when giving prophecy is because, *"The testimony of Jesus is the spirit of prophecy"* (Revelation 19:10).

When people act irresponsibly, they damage the testimony of Jesus. The person speaking is accountable for the use, abuse, control or suppression of this gift.

When people give a word based on their own perceptions, desires or even misunderstanding, they undermine the testimony of Jesus and any ministry the Lord may have intended for them. People will not believe them after they hear false messages given in the name of the Lord. Their very words will neutralize their credibility from that time forward. *"Having therefore these promises dearly beloved, let us cleanse ourselves from all filthiness of the flesh and spirit, perfecting holiness in the fear of God"* (II Corinthians 7:1). The vessels of God must be as clean as possible.

False prophets are people who speak words tainted by the devil or the works of the flesh. They may say they are speaking for the Lord, but their message does not conform to the written Word of God and usually the fruit of the Spirit are absent in their life. Quite often the fruit they do have are filled with confusion and chaos. In 2 Chronicles 18:18-22, the Bible teaches how the false prophets had allowed lying spirits to come into their mouths and use them. Their compromise with lying spirits ultimately caused their captivity.

A true word of prophecy gives a small insight into God's vast will for people's lives. A valid prophecy will never contradict the written Word of God but will complement it. *"But the word of the Lord endureth forever. And this is the word which by the gospel is preached unto you"* (1 Peter 1:25).

The prophecy of Joel 2:28-32 was quoted by Peter on the day of Pentecost when the Holy Spirit baptized them and said, *"I will pour out of my Spirit upon all flesh: and your sons and your daughters shall prophesy"* (Acts 2:17). This has been fulfilled through the ages by men and women that God has used as His mouthpiece. Philip had four virgin daughters who all prophesied (John 14;3). There is gender equality as far as the Holy Spirit is concerned when it comes to spiritual callings and anointing. *"There is neither Jew nor Greek, there is neither bond nor free, there is neither male nor female: for ye are all one in Christ Jesus"* (Galatians 3:28).   *a ch 21:9+14*

A greater acceptance of the gift of prophecy is being found in the church today and according to scripture, it will be more prominent as the end of this age draws closer.

A person who gives a prophecy does not necessarily fill the office or ministry calling of a prophet. The prophecy given as a gift of the Holy Spirit can come on all those who have the faith to prophesy. *"For ye may all prophesy one by one, that all may learn, and all may be comforted"* (I Corinthians 14:31). The main ingredient to being used by the Holy Spirit in this area is to be willing and quickly obedient to speak out what the Spirit would like to say.

New converts can prophesy when the Holy Spirit baptizes them. *"When Paul had laid his hands upon them, the Holy Ghost came on them; and they spake with tongues, and prophesied"* (Acts 19:6). These new converts spoke out the wonderful works of God by prophecy.

Gifts of Grace

The gifts of God are not the personal property of someone who has logged on forty-five years of faithful service. They are the gifts of grace given by the Holy Spirit to any believer who wants them. The goal of each believer should always be to please God in everything and excel in all the gifts.

When a word of prophecy is given, the body of Christ should always listen and consider carefully the spoken message. *"Quench not the Spirit. Despise not prophesyings. Prove all things; hold fast that which is good"* (I Thessalonians 5:19-21).

The instruction is just as valid for today because we need prophetic voices to speak clearly the will of God. Prophecy is not an infallible word and therefore the church must cautiously judge the prophetic word and hold fast to the things that apply. The church wants all God has for them, but she does not want or need, any more error (I Corinthians 14:29,32; I John 4:1, I Thessalonians 5:20-21).

The gift of prophecy very often works with the gifts of a word of wisdom or a word of knowledge. Sometimes it is difficult to distinguish between them.

How Is Prophecy Judged?

Because the Gift of Prophecy did not begin on the day of Pentecost like tongues and interpretation of tongues, there are certain rules that govern the contents of prophecy in both the Old and New Testaments. The only thing that changed was the fact that God is willing to entrust each believer with His gifts of the Holy Spirit today. Everyone can prophesy according to the faith that works in them.

Scripture shows God's prophets sometimes got away from the will of God and spoke out of their own hearts. They needed correction. Just as in those days of old, there will always be people using the gifts for their own gain, trying to manipulate churches and individuals with them. There will always be wolves trying to divide the flock.

Each person giving a prophetic word should be accountable to others who are seasoned in the Word of God and the gifts of the Spirit. If correction is needed, those who are listening and judging the prophecy should administer the correction in love and compassion. *"Let the prophets speak two or three, and let the others judge"* (I Corinthians 14:29).

Correction should never be brutal. The truth must be spoken in love (Eph.4:15). If a person continues to prophecy falsely, they need to be disciplined and taught by those to whom they are accountable.

"And the word of the LORD came unto me, saying, Son of man, prophesy against the prophets of Israel that prophesy, and say thou unto them that prophesy out of their own hearts, Hear ye the word of

55

THE GIFTS OF THE HOLY SPIRIT ARE FOR YOU!

the LORD; thus saith the Lord GOD; Woe unto the foolish prophets, that follow their own spirit, and have seen nothing! O Israel, thy prophets are like the foxes in the deserts. Ye have not gone up into the gaps, neither made up the hedge for the house of Israel to stand in the battle in the day of the LORD. They have seen vanity and lying divination, saying the LORD saith: and the LORD hath not sent them: and they have made others to hope that they would confirm the word. Have ye not seen a vain vision, and have ye not spoken a lying divination, whereas ye say, The LORD saith it; albeit I have not spoken? Therefore thus saith the Lord GOD; Because ye have spoken vanity, and seen lies, therefore, behold, I am against you, saith the Lord GOD. And mine hand shall be upon the prophets that see vanity, that divine lies: they shall not be in the assembly of my people, . . and ye shall know that I am the Lord GOD" (Ezekiel 13:1-9).

"Then the Lord said unto me, The prophets prophesy lies in my name: I sent them not, neither have I commanded them, neither spake unto them: they prophesy unto you a false vision and divination, and a thing of nought, and the deceit of their heart." Jeremiah 14:14

"And if thou say in thine heart, How shall we know the word which the Lord hath not spoken? When a prophet speaketh in the name of the Lord, if the thing follow not, nor come to pass, that is the thing which the Lord hath not spoken, but the prophet hath spoken it presumptuously: thou shalt not be afraid of him" (Deuteronomy 18:21,22).

God will never bring confusion or contradiction of His written Word through a word of prophecy. The Holy Spirit, who gives the gift of prophecy will never contradict scripture. He was the one who inspired it to be written. Scripture always brings balance to what we see and hear. *"All scripture is given by inspiration of God, and is profitable for doctrine, for reproof, for correction, for instruction in righteousness":* (II Timothy 3:16).

It is God's written Word that is the deciding factor when it comes to defining whether a prophecy is true or false. Doctrine does not come through prophecy, it is already established by God's written Word.

If a prophetic utterance is given that is futuristic, it must happen just as the speaker has said or that person has given a false prophecy and no one need listen to them anymore.

Satan will try to use carnal believers or even satanic plants within the church to give false prophecies. When a false prophetic word goes unchallenged by anyone, it will cause division and confusion. God is not the author of confusion, so the only other sources are the devil or carnal human desires. There are people who have a hard time believing that the devil will try to interfere with a church service or gathering of believers, but we are warned about such problems and are challenged to be on guard. *"Beloved, believe not every spirit, but try the spirits whether they are of God: because many false prophets are gone out into the world"* (I John 4:1).

The Word of God is sharper than any two-edged sword and is fully able to divide between the things of the soul (fleshly desires) and the things of the spirit (Hebrews 4:12). Each person is admonished to study the Word of God so thoroughly they become laborers that do not need to be ashamed. The stronger a person gets in the knowledge and wisdom of God's Word, the more he can discern when there are false prophecies or any other thing hindering the work of God. *"But strong meat belongeth to them that are of full age, even those who by reason of use have their senses exercised to discern both good and evil"* (Hebrews 5:14).

It is the responsibility of each believer to know that his heart is right with God and he is walking in the revelation of God's Word. God wants each to excel in the gifts, but He also holds the individual accountable. Satan is aware of how the gifts should be used. He has tripped up many sincere persons who learned how to let the gifts flow but did not take time to study the Word. As a result, he brought shame to the body of Christ.

Prophecy Will Confirm God's Will

Paul and Barnabas knew from their own prayer time with God that He had called them to do the work of apostles. He confirmed this calling in the presence of other witnesses. *"As they ministered to the Lord, and fasted, the Holy Ghost said, Separate me Barnabas and Saul for the work whereunto I have called them"* (Acts 13:2).

Prophecy can confirm a call or word of direction that God has already spoken to an individual's spirit. When this happens, the Holy

Spirit bears witness in the individual's spirit and brings an immediate confirmation that they have heard from God.

Believers should beware of prophetic words given about future direction or ministries God has not called them into first. These need to be taken into prayerful consideration and not acted on in haste. God will always take time to train people when He calls them.

A lady once received a prophecy saying she was to be in a ministry. She immediately quit her job to fulfill the call. However, no ministry opened and her finances dwindled precariously. She was counseled to go back to her job and told to wait on the Lord's timing for ministry doors to open. She was also told God would use the interim time to train her so when, and if, doors of ministry opened she would be well prepared. The lady immediately sensed peace and wisdom in this counsel. She realized she had been too hasty.

God always has a training time for people He calls into the ministry. Even Paul spent thirteen years in training as he waited for God to open ministry opportunities for him.

The Vessel

If a bucket of water has dirty rocks in it, when the water is poured off it is muddy. It would not be fit to drink.

In the same way, human beings are the vessels of the Holy Spirit. There needs to be a continual cleansing action so when the Holy Spirit pours through us, He is not tainted by any uncleanness.

"And we beseech you, brethren, to know them which labour among you, and are over you in the Lord, and admonish you"; (I Thessalonians 5:12). It is very important to know the ones who come into a congregation or group and minister words that they say are from the Lord. Someone should know them or their spiritual pedigree. What kind of ministry do they have? If a stranger is really anointed of God and tempered in maturity, he will take the time to be known of the group before he attempts any ministry. Very soon, the gifts resident in him will make room for him to minister.

Much of the time the Holy Spirit's message of prophecy is given to draw the community into a worshipful response to God.

In the Old Testament we can draw out an illustration from when God sent manna from heaven daily to feed His people. It became wormy and smelly if they tried to use it for another day unless they were specifically directed to do so. A word of prophecy written down and reread later can be a blessing to the person who recieved it. But, normally, God gives a fresh word [or manna] for the moment. A prophecy written down and shared outside its original context will often be out of its season and lose the impact it had. Discernment should be gotten before sharing any word of prophecy outside the place and time of its revelation.

Sometimes God directs people to write prophetic words and give them to a specific person as God gives the right timing. These are often to be used as a confirmation of something He has been speaking to them about. These can be an encouragement, etc. as that person receives the words and knows God was aware of them.

Others may want to record or write words of the prophecy down to review them later so they remember the exact wording of the en-couragement, etc. given to them.

God made His gifts of the Spirit available to the church for His definite purposes. They were not given for entertainment. God's gifts should never become common and yet He wants to lavish them on the church as they are needed to encourage, lift up the believer and bring correction and edification to the church.

Sometimes a lack of understanding God's Word and how He works has caused people to push for revelations so hard they speak out the desires of their own heart. These people need more teaching on the use and abuse of the gifts of the Holy Spirit. If spiritual bless-ings are desired for a person, its not wrong to ask God for them. However, it is wrong to make it sound like God is saying it when He's not.

"The teaching of I Corinthians suggest the prophet can be wrong, but error would not necessarily brand the prophet as false. Recogniz-ing that error can be present in the message of any human prophet today should be the safeguard against being swept into foolish or unwise actions advocated by a 'prophetic word.' False prophets exist (I John 4:1,3) and can be exposed by the gift of 'discerning of spirits' (I Corinthians 12:10) and the scriptural test of 1 Corinthians 12:3 and I John 4:2,3.

"Recognizing that error can be present in the message of any human prophet today should be the safeguard against being swept into foolish or unwise actions advocated by a 'prophetic word.'" (Carlson, Aug. 1990, p. 4.)

A person should never act hastily on the basis of an uncon-firmed prediction or directed prophecy regardless of how inspired it might sound at the moment. Any words directed to an individual are usually as a confirmation to what God has already been speaking to their heart, they are not to give arbitrary or absolute direction. So-called moral directives or personal guidance given as prophetic words that are not confirmed by scripture is not binding on the believer's life.

With all prophecies, we need to ask where it originated? Did it glorify man or God? What did it produce, confusion or peace? Did it produce pride in anyone? Did it come from personal desires or from God? Did it exalt Christ? Did it produce liberty or bondage?

"We judge the prophecy, not the prophet. "This weighing would not judge between false prophets and true prophets, or between those under demonic control or those directed by the Spirit, but whether the prophecy was scripturally correct or valid for the circumstance. The tests spoken of in I Corinthians 14:29 and I Thessalonians 5:19-21 are for the purpose of evaluating the prophecies of those who are accepted as believers in the assembly. The prophet's words — not the prophet himself — are judged" (Carlson, Aug. 5, 1990, p. 4.).

Jesus gave us all the right to be fruit inspectors in Matthew 7:15-20. By judging fruit, we look to see whether the fruit is good or bad and then we'll know the source.

Human beings are not always perfect. When people first begin to speak the ideas God has given, they need to be reminded they are speaking for God and are not free to embellish the message with their own thoughts in any way or it will detract from the message and start them on a dangerous path just like the false prophets of old. We need to grow as Jesus did when he, *"increased in wisdom and stat-ure, and in favor with God and man"* (Luke 2:52).

A prophecy does not take the form of condemnation. It can, however, be given as spiritual counsel to correct doctrinal error, etc. This should be the truth spoken in love as the Holy Spirit does His necessary work. The Holy Spirit will often bring a conviction on the hearts of the listeners to respond to the correction.

Satan is the accuser of the brethren (Revelation 12:10). He condemns and harshly accuses believers day and night. He will bring a spirit of heaviness with him and try to neutralize the faith of those listening. Prophecies of a harsh, critical nature that threaten people do not originate in the Spirit of Christ. They come from either the devil or man's own critical spirit.

Those in leadership need to be quick to discern if there is error among the body of Christ and correct it or weed it out. There is no room to hesitate. If a word has been spoken that does not live up to the letter of God's Word, it needs to be judged and thrown out as worthless.

THE GIFTS OF THE HOLY SPIRIT ARE FOR YOU!

"The Word of our God stands forever."
Isaiah 40:8

Diagram 8:1

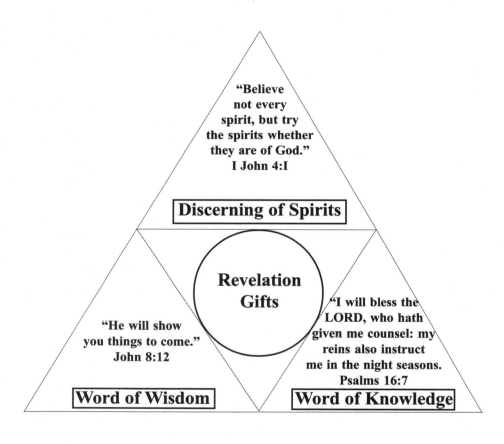

**"I will teach thee and instruct thee
in the way which thou shalt go." Psalms 32:8**

CHAPTER 8

THE WORD OF KNOWLEDGE

The word of knowledge brings a small piece of divine intelligence to the human level by the power of the Holy Spirit, allowing a person to know the supernatural mind of God about something. God has all knowledge. He is omniscient. He has all the data that pertain to things in heaven and on earth, including persons and spirit beings. He is conscious of their status always, simultaneously. He knows about everything, every person and every place both in existence and out of existence. This is not because God just has a good memory, God has all these facts before Him all the time. God is always in the present but He looks at the past, present and future like we look at the present. Where we can only see some facts in front of us or behind us, God sees all activity everywhere simultaneously.

The Greek Definition of the Word of Knowledge

"Word," taken from the Greek, "lógos," means "to announce or report from some place or person; then, to announce, report, or publish something that has happened, been experienced, or heard" (A Critical Lexicon and Concordance to the English and Greek New Testament, 1979, p. 898). The word, "knowledge," from the Greek, "gnosis," means "knowing, or recognition, the knowledge or understanding of a thing, the insight which manifests itself in the thorough understanding of the subjects with which it meets and in the conduct determined thereby"; (Ibid, p. 436). A further rendering would be: "The power of knowing, intelligence, comprehension. Subjectively spoken of what one knows, knowledge" (The Complete Word Study Dictionary New Testament, 1993, p. 378.). In this case, the knowledge known is supernatural and brings to the present, information about the past, present and future from the archives of God.

The gift of the Word of Knowledge is the revelation to man by God's Spirit of some detail of the great wealth of knowledge God possesses. The wording of this gift is significant. It is the "word" of knowledge. It is not all that God knows, it is just a word, or a particle, of His great knowledge. To our limited minds those small bits seem like great revelations when in fact they are only a small speck of all that God knows about the subject.

The word of knowledge is given by an inner witness of the Holy Spirit and may or may not be spoken audibly, depending on the direction of the Holy Spirit to the individual who has received it.

A person can take these fragments and sometimes expend a lifetime trying to explain the revelations adequately to others because they have so revolutionized their thinking on a subject. Mankind cannot even begin to imagine how vast the mind of God is.

Christians have been promised the mind of Christ in 1 Corinthians 2:16 *"For who has known the mind of the Lord that he may instruct Him? But we have the mind of Christ" (Also see Phil 2:5).* Adding to that then, He has given us the gift of the Word of Knowledge where He adds little bits and pieces of His wonderful, unsearchable Knowledge. It is up to the individual to receive it and use it properly. Jesus said that He would send the Holy Spirit to teach us all things (John 14:26).

Where it concerns the gifts of God, our minds are not in any way connected to the gifts of God. They are not an amplification of human knowledge. It is a divinely given fragment of divine knowledge. We cannot acquire it by study or concentration. A word of knowledge is a flash of divine revelation concerning things that were hopelessly hidden from the senses, mind and natural thoughts of mankind. Man contributes nothing and receives everything. Age, education and nationality make no difference to the working of this gift. It is a miracle of the Holy Spirit. Through the word of knowledge, the whole realm of God's facts is at a person's disposal as the Spirit wills them to be.

The Word of Knowledge Is a Powerful Weapon

The word of knowledge is revealed throughout the Old and New Testaments. It continues today as a useful tool in the hand of an Omniscient God who trusts His people with some of His knowledge. The Holy Spirit usually reveals a word of knowledge to people so they can change a condition by prayer, spiritual warfare or whatever other action the Spirit directs them to take. The word of knowledge is a powerful weapon against the power of the devil.

This supernatural revelation of knowledge may reveal the condition of a person's thoughts, heart, a physical condition, actions, or it may give information about objects and places, etc.

One of Satan's counterfeits for this is called "mind-reading." However, there is no such thing as mind-reading, by the devil or his followers because scripture tells us that only God knows the heart and mind of man. God only reveals things as the Holy Spirit feels it is necessary in time of need (Deuteronomy 29:29; I Kings 8:39; I Chronicles 28:9; Daniel 2:20-23; Amos 4:13; Psalms 147:4,5; Psalms 94:11; Proverbs 15:3; Isaiah 29:15-16; 40:28; Ezekiel 11:5; Luke 16:5; Acts 15:18; Hebrews 4:12,13; Romans 8:27; Romans 11:33-36; I Corinthians 2:10-12; I Corinthians 3:19,20; Jeremiah 17: 9,10; Ecclesiastes 12:14; I John 3:20; Revelation 2:23).

People who promote themselves as mind-readers are people who are being fed information by a spirit of divination or a familiar spirit that are mentioned in the Bible. These spirits know a certain amount of superficial things about a person, but when it comes to the mind of man, only God has the capability to know his thoughts. Only God can give divine knowledge about things.

Isaiah 14 and Ezekiel 28 mention that Lucifer (Satan) had wisdom and knowledge, but he is just a created being (an angel), and as such has only limited wisdom. He does not possess God's supernatural knowledge. Satan and his demons can only observe and listen to gain the advantage over mankind. His thinking has the same earthly process as mankind's has . . . he is not divine (Matthew 16:23).

Through the word of knowledge, the Church may be purified, the distressed comforted, the saint gladdened, lost property recovered, Satan defeated and the Lord Jesus glorified. It reveals the condition of things.

THE GIFTS OF THE HOLY SPIRIT ARE FOR YOU!

Each gift has its own purpose for existing and should not be confused with another, nor can it be replaced by another.

The Word of Knowledge is given by an inner witness of the Holy Spirit. It should only be shared with others when the Holy Spirit instructs us to do so. The word of knowledge is shared as a direct act of faith as God supplies the thoughts. It can also be revealed to a person without an unction to speak it. The word of wisdom will direct a person to speak or guard the word of knowledge.

Mary Was Given Revelation Knowledge

Mary was given revelation about the life of Jesus before and after he was born but the Bible tells us that she guarded these revelations in her heart. *"But Mary kept all these things, and pondered them in her heart"* (Luke 2:19). Throughout the years she thought about and pondered those things and we do not know if she ever shared any of them with other people. She observed Jesus as he grew into manhood and his unusual ministry. She was among the hundred and twenty gathered in the upper room on the day of Pentecost. She obviously believed her son was the Son of God and wanted to be there to receive all that He had to give His followers.

Revelation knowledge was given to Mary by the angel Gabriel, and confirmed through the mouths of other reputable people of that day such as Simeon and Anna the prophetess (Luke 2:25-38), also her cousin Elizabeth and the shepherds and wise men.

Another example of the Word of Knowledge is John the Revelator when he was in the spirit during his exile on the Isle of Patmos. He was given knowledge of the condition of the seven churches of Asia (Revelation 2 and 3). There was no way in the natural that he could have known the condition of the seven churches. There were no communication services between him and the mainland. He was in total isolation. The only way he could have come into this kind of knowledge was because of divine revelation. He warned them of their spiritual condition. Many church members of that day probably did not even recognize the actual condition of their churches, yet John could document it because the Holy Spirit was revealing it to him. We recognize some of our own church conditions in those same writings today.

Knowledge in the King's Chambers

Another example of the word of knowledge is found in 2 Kings 6:8-12 when the Syrian king was attempting to make war against Israel. Elisha kept the Israelites so well informed by the Word of Knowledge from the Lord that the king of Syria thought there was a spy in his bedroom listening to his private conversations. Things he had only spoken in secret were being revealed openly.

"Then the king of Syria warred against Israel, and took counsel with his servants, saying, In such and such a place shall be my camp. And the man of God sent unto the king of Israel, saying, Beware that thou pass not such a place; for thither the Syrians are come down. And the king of Israel sent to the place which the man of God told him and warned him of, and saved himself there, not once nor twice. Therefore the heart of the king of Syria was sore troubled for this thing; and he called his servants, and said unto them, Will ye not shew me which of us is for the king of Israel? And one of his servants said, None, my lord, O king: but Elisha, the prophet that is in Israel, telleth the king of Israel the words that thou speakest in thy bedchamber."

The Word of Knowledge was revealing the enemy's tactics. As people search the scriptures and spend time in God's presence many times the Holy Spirit will reveal ahead of time what the enemy has planned for destruction so the believer can block him in prayer.

One day the Holy Spirit told me to pray for a woman who's husband was diagnosed to have cancer. She was under an attack by a spirit of fear. The Holy Spirit told me to stand against the enemy and break the power of the attack. This lady very seldom called me but about a half hour after I prayed she called requesting prayer. She said she had been under such an attack from fear and needed prayer because she didn't want to let her husband see her in this condition. I told her the Lord had already told me I was to pray for her and her husband earlier that morning. As we prayed together on the phone, she said she could feel the grip of fear turn loose and back off from her.

The Holy Spirit had spoken to me to take time earlier to pray for her and He also spoke to her heart to contact me so we could agree together in prayer. Matthew 18:19,20 tells us the importance

67

of two people agreeing so their prayers will be answered. *"Again I say to you that if two of you agree on earth concerning anything that they ask, it will be done for them by My Father in heaven. For where two or three are gathered together in My name, I am there in the midst of them."*

This is a present day illustration of how God can give a Word of Knowledge so we can counterattack the enemy before he can win a victory.

Saul's Conversion

After Saul was converted on the Damascus road, everyone was afraid of him but God spoke to Ananias. He told him in great detail where Saul was. He spoke of the street, the house, his thoughts, his attitude and his future ministry in Acts 9:11,12. *"So the Lord said to him, 'Arise and go to the street called Straight, and inquire at the house of Judas for one called Saul of Tarsus, for behold, he is praying. And in a vision he has seen a man named Ananias coming in and putting his hand on him, so that he might receive his sight.'"*

This came by a Word of Knowledge. After Ananias received this, he was encouraged to go pray for Saul and nothing would harm him. In fact, he was told that Saul would gladly receive him and all he had to offer. Saul did exactly as the Holy Spirit indicated, he responded and received all that God had for him through Ananias's ministry.

Before this, Saul would have thrown Ananias in jail and persecuted him. But when Saul was ready to listen and receive, the Holy Spirit knew the right timing and spoke to Ananias, sending him to be the instrument of God's perfect plan in Saul's life. If we wait patiently on the Lord for His perfect timing concerning that "impossible person" we have been praying about, God's Holy Spirit will tell us the exact moment to take action for them. He will let us know if we are to take the salvation message to them or pray that the Lord will send someone else to minister to them (Lk. 10:2).

We not only need the word of knowledge, but we also need the word of wisdom to tell us just when and how to do it. These two gifts usually work together.

Peter and the Gentiles

Peter after his vision in Acts 10:19 concerning the gentiles, was told that there would be three men waiting at his gate to see him. When he descended from the rooftop, he was told the three men had just arrived at the gate. This Word of Knowledge was very important for Peter because until this time, he really had no interest in gentiles. He was not concerned about reaching the gentile nations with the gospel. He was a Jew and he was going to stay a good Jew and not mix with the heathen. Until now Peter had considered all gentiles unclean and unfit for the kingdom of God.

As Peter was thinking about the vision, a word of knowledge came to him about the men at the gate. He was only told to go with them. He was not told any more details about what was going to happen. If he had known all the facts, it is possible that Peter would have refused to obey the Holy Spirit's voice. God used him in this situation to start the outreach to the gentiles. He was obedient to the Spirit of God. If he had not chosen to obey, he would not have seen the rest of the revelation and the ensuing results at the house of Cornelius.

It is one thing to receive a revelation from God, it is another thing to walk it out and be obedient. How many times do each of us receive a nudging of the Holy Spirit to do something and we pull back from it? Through intimidation the devil causes us to shrink back and we refuse to respond to what the Holy Spirit has spoken to us.

We must learn to respond and be obedient. We should never purposely ignore the Holy Spirit's voice. It is disobedience. When we grieve the Holy Spirit we must ask God for forgiveness for the lost times and request new challenges. Over and over again God will present new opportunities. Be prompt to respond. If not, you are making a decision for God in the matter.

If you want to see people saved, healed and set free from bondages the Lord will direct your paths with His great revelation knowledge and wisdom.

As with all the gifts of the Spirit, a person must ask, believe, receive by faith and trust God to use them when the need arises and yield in faith to the anointing or prompting.

You are only an instrument of God. He wants to work through

you and bless other people as you make yourself available.

Reveals Hypocrisy

The gift of the word of knowledge can be used to reveal hypocrisy. Gehazi, in 2 Kings 5:20-27, thought he could collect some loot from Naaman after he was healed of leprosy. Naaman was so thankful for his healing he would have given away anything and Gehazi took advantage of that. He followed Naaman in secret and asked for payment, thinking the Elisha was not profiting enough from the situation. Naaman decided to deceitfully profit from what had been offered Elisha. He wanted to secretly gain what had been offered to the profet.

God's genuine messengers do not charge for the gifts of God. There should be no price put on the value of prayer. An answer to prayer is not a matter of merchandise, it is a gift of God that is freely given. Humanity does not meet the need, they only make the request. God is the giver.

Elisha recognized this truth and did not charge Naaman or anyone else for his services. He told Naaman he did not want his gold, silver and clothing. God had other ways of supplying Elisha's livelihood. When he found out by the Holy Spirit that his servant went behind his back and took the loot Gehazi became leprous and Elisha banished him. The Word of Knowledge exposed his deceit.

Deception Is Revealed

A New Testament illustration of deception is the account of Ananias and Saphira (Acts 5:1-11). They lied to the disciples, the apostolic church and the Holy Spirit. They declared they had sold their belongings and were giving all the money to the church. They had the right to sell their properties and give whatever percentage they wanted to the church. They were not forced to give 100 percent, they could have saved back whatever portion they wanted to for their own use. They wanted the attention and glory for something that was not the truth. They were not just lying to the people involved, they were lying to the Holy Spirit.

Remember John 4:24 tells us, *"God is Spirit, and those who worship Him must worship in spirit and truth."* They were trying to worship God with their money using falsehood. The Holy Spirit revealed the truth by a word of knowledge to Peter who exposed them. The enemy was able to take advantage of their unconfessed sin and kill them on the spot.

The revelation of sin in their heart was a very serious thing to God. Sin created a wide-open door in their lives and the results illustrated how the enemy gained a victory over them.

Jesus Knew Her Whole Life

Jesus astounded the woman at the well in John 4:1-26, when he told her all about her past and present life. She thought he was reading her mind but Jesus assured her that His revelation was from God.

Often we read in scripture that Jesus knew their thoughts. How did he know them? He knew through the revelation of the word of knowledge by the Holy Spirit. Many times he would answer the thoughts of the scribes and Pharisees directly, surprising them by His insight to their thoughts. Only the mind of God can know the thoughts and intents of the heart and reveal them to mankind.

We as humans can see reactions and hear words spoken or even observe body language of others and make fair guesses at what they are thinking. It is still different. The knowledge that we're studying about is from the mind of God. When Jesus spoke those things to the woman at the well they were not to condemn her but to help her know God knew about her and still cared for her. Jesus let her know God even loved the Samaritans.

She was amazed a real prophet of God would talk to her or allow her to pull up water and serve him a drink. Normally a man of God would not go into the territory of the Samaritans or in any way contaminate themselves by touching anything of a Samaritan. They would never eat anything from the hand of a Samaritan woman.

This was not even an ordinary good woman of Samaria. She was considered a woman of the streets. She had a procession of lovers and husbands. The one she was now living with was not her husband. She did not come to the well early in the morning with the rest of the women of the community. She came later in the day because she was not socially accepted.

Jesus revealed to her who He was. When she realized what He

was saying to her, she began to accept Him and all that He had done. When she heard about the water of life that was being offered to her, her first thought was to run back to her city and tell everyone that would listen to her about this wonderful discovery.

Often while visiting with someone, the Holy Spirit will bring revelation knowledge to our mind about things that we would never have any way of knowing. Some of them are incorporated into conversation without making a conscious effort to say them and yet they stir the heart of the one listening. Sometimes it brings conviction about hidden areas but it is accompanied with an assurance that God really cares about them.

As we read the Bible we see that the word of knowledge was very active in both the Old and New Testament.

Today's Ministry of the Word of Knowledge

Many people have been used of God to speak a Word of Knowledge to help another receive a physical healing. They will describe not only the person but what their ailment is that God wants to heal.

On the mission field, I was called one day by a mother to pray for her two college age children who had declared that they were taking time off from serving God to live as they wanted for a year. When I arrived, I could see it was obvious they were not there voluntarily. I visited with them for a little while and then asked if I could pray for them as their mother had requested. They grudgingly agreed but I could see from the look that passed between them, they had already exchanged some doubts about this whole situation.

As I started to pray for the girl, the Lord began to show me some details about her life to let her know He really had a personal interest in the details of her life. I asked her how long she had been suffering from stomach pains?

She looked at me and said,"Who told you that?"

I said, "The Holy Spirit has shown me this but I'll pray now that it'll be healed if you really want me to."

She was healed that day and began to serve the Lord with her whole heart.

Another time whle praying for a lady, the shape of a stomach with a sore on it was revealed. The Lord immediately healed her of an ulcer after prayer.

The Holy Spirit even slips in words of knowledge when we're not always aware of them. One day while teaching about the gifts of the Spirit I was explaining the word of knowledge and how the late Katherine Kuhlman was used as an instrument of the Holy Spirit to tell people of their healing. I explained that if Miss Kuhlman were there that day she would tell the third person in on the fifth row to stand because she was just then being healed of a gall bladder problem and could feel a warm heat going through her body.

To my amazement, the third woman on the fifth row jumped up clutching her side and exclaimed that she could feel the heat and was being healed of a gall bladder problem that she had been suffering from for several weeks.

God wants to use us even in the natural course of our daily activity. He wants to give us the gifts of His Spirit without limitation. He holds us responsible for studying so we know what to do with them. Possibly, we are to intercede privately because of what the revelation has shown, or maybe we are share the information with others. He will let us know if we wait for His word of wisdom concerning the gift.

The important thing to know is that He wants each to make themselves available to Him.

THE GIFTS OF THE HOLY SPIRIT ARE FOR YOU!

CHAPTER 9

THE WORD OF WISDOM

The word of wisdom is a revelation of the divine will of God received by hearing the voice of the Spirit. It comes through dreams, visions or insight, a deep impression, a witness of the Spirit, scripture or by the vocal gifts, concerning people, things or events. It can be spoken in prophecy or counsel. This gift often works with the gift of the word of knowledge, prophecy or tongues and interpretation of tongues. Whenever a person receives the gift of a word of knowledge or discerning of spirits, he or she should also wait on the Lord to find out His wisdom on when or how to use that word.

All true words of wisdom and knowledge come from God. They are available to all believers who wish to ask for them. *"In whom are hid all the treasures of wisdom and knowledge"* (Colossians 2:3). *"If any of you lack wisdom, let him ask of God, that giveth to all men liberally, and upbraideth not; and it shall be given him. But let him ask in faith, nothing wavering. For he that wavereth is like a wave of the sea driven with the wind and tossed."* ~James 1, 5, 6.~

In God's immeasurable mind all the information about the universe is viewed as a current fact. He also sees through the eons of time and eternity, present, past and future which culminates in His infinite Wisdom. When God reveals a glance into His time and personal data bank with mankind, He is giving them a Word of Wisdom.

This supernatural Word of Wisdom is revealed by the Holy Spirit to the spirit and mind of a person. It reveals the wonderful purposes

75

and Will of God pertaining to people, places, things, societies and nations.

The Word of Wisdom is communicated by God giving people commands and instructions as well as in foretelling future events out of His infinite knowledge of what will take place.

In the Greek the word *wisdom*, is *sophia* it means complete or superior intelligence. This wisdom has the ability to say and do the right thing in the right way at the right time. Sometimes it comes as an instant understanding of how to do something or apply some knowledge that God has already given a person.

Dr. Spiros Zodiates defines divine wisdom as follows: "In respect to divine things, wisdom, knowledge, insight, deep understanding, represented everywhere as a divine gift, and including the idea of practical application. *Sophia* stands for divine wisdom, the ability to regulate one's relationship with God. and is distinct from *phronesis* (Strong's #5428), prudence, the ability to know and deal with people (1 Cor. 12:8; Eph. 1:17; Col. 1:9); 2 Peter 3:15). Specifically of insight imparted from God in respect to the divine counsels (1 Cor. 2:6,7). Metonymically of the author and source of this wisdom (1 Cor. 1:30). As conjoined with purity of heart and life (James 1:5; 3:13,15,17).

"The wisdom of God means the divine wisdom, including the ideas of infinite skill, insight, knowledge, purity (Rom. 11:33; 1 Cor. 1:21,24; Eph. 3:10; Col 2:3; Rev. 5:12; 7:12). Of the divine wisdom as revealed and manifested in Christ and His gospel (Matt. 11:19; Luke 7:35; 11:49)" (The Complete Word Study Dictionary New Testament, 1993, p. 1301).

This gift has nothing to do with natural ability or learning. It is supernatural wisdom. It is the *word* for the given situation in question from the vast reserves of wisdom that belong to God.

Paul displayed that it was God's will for all believers to have divine wisdom when he prayed for the saints at Ephesus, *"That the God of our Lord Jesus Christ, the Father of glory, may give unto you the spirit of wisdom and revelation in the knowledge of him"*: (Ephesians 1:17). Again, we see this attitude revealed to the saints at Colossae. *"For this cause we also, since the day we heard it, do not cease to pray for you, and to desire that ye might be filled with the knowledge of his will in all wisdom and spiritual understanding";* (Colossians 1:9).

James explains the difference between divine wisdom and devilish, worldly wisdom: *"Who is a wise man and endued with knowledge among you? let him show out of a good conversation his works with meekness of wisdom. But if ye have bitter envying and strife in your hearts, glory not, and lie not against the truth. This wisdom descendeth not from above, but is earthly, sensual, devilish. For where envying and strife is, there is confusion and every evil work. But the wisdom that is from above is first pure, then peaceable, gentle, and easy to be entreated, full of mercy and good fruits, without partiality, and without hypocrisy, And the fruit of righteousness is sown in peace of them that make peace"* (James 3:13-18).

This passage demonstrates the three types of wisdom. First, we see God's great storehouse of wisdom that has no limitations and results in peace, mercy and good fruits to everyone who applies it. Secondly, man's wisdom is shown, based on sensual desires and carnal knowledge. Third, Satan's wisdom surfaces and brings strife, confusion and evil results.

Human knowledge has a tendency to cause people to say the wrong things because of a natural limitation of all the facts at hand. Because of saying the wrong thing at the wrong time, people spend years trying to justify or correct the words spoken in haste. This very thing often places a gulf between two people for years if it is not taken care of properly.

A word of wisdom from God, has the divine nature of God wrapped up in it and never hurts people. It will bring peace when it is spoken in love and mercy. When a person pursues the direction God has given through a word of wisdom the situation is resolved with good results and blessings.

The book of Proverbs is dedicated to teaching us about the importance of having and using God's wisdom. *"Happy is the man that findeth wisdom, and the man that getteth understanding: for the merchandise of it is better than the merchandise of silver, and the gain thereof than fine gold. She is more precious than rubies; and all the things thou canst desire are not to be compared unto her. Length of days is in her right hand; and in her left hand riches and honor. Her ways are ways of pleasantness, and all her paths are peace. She is a tree of life to them that lay hold upon her: and happy is every one that retaineth her. The Lord by wisdom hath founded the earth; by understanding hath he established the heavens. By his knowledge the depths are broken up, and the clouds drop down the dew. My son, let not them depart from thine eyes: keep sound wisdom and discretion: so shall they be life unto thy soul, and grace to thy neck. Then shalt thou walk in thy way safely, and thy foot shall not stumble"* (Proverbs 3:13-23).

The world market price of silver, gold and precious stones constantly fluctuates up and down. Divine wisdom is better than the gold market, it only goes up in value. Rubies are one of the scarcest gems available to mankind and yet wisdom is finer than the best rubies ever dug out of the earth. Real Godly wisdom is a rare commodity offered to mankind liberally from the Holy Spirit.

"For wisdom is better than rubies; and all the things that may be desired are not to be compared to it" (Proverbs 8:11). Solomon had all the silver, gold and precious stones anyone could ever want in his day and still advocated that wisdom from God is of greater value than any earthly substance.

The gift of the word of wisdom is one of the most useful gifts given. This is the gift that can give direction in times of crisis. If people would wait for God and give Him a chance to speak it would save many a person from hitting the wall spiritually or traveling around the same mountain seventy-seven times without being able to speak to it.

The word of wisdom has nothing to do with natural ability. It is entirely supernatural. God is the only source of this supernatural wisdom. It cannot be absorbed out of library books or the halls of learning.

During a time of crisis, Jesus said believers would be supernaturally given words of wisdom that will astound the accusers. *Settle it therefore in your hearts, not to meditate before what ye shall answer: For I will give you a mouth and wisdom which all your adversaries shall not be able to gainsay nor resist"* (Luke 21:14-15).

Jesus practiced this instruction when he was questioned about His authority by the chief priests and elders. He answered them with a question. Jesus always knew exactly what to say. In this instance, His question was used to silence his attackers (Matt. 21:23-27).

When the Pharisees tried to entrap Jesus in a dilemma concerning payment of tribute to Caesar, Jesus put a stop to their argument and caused them to marvel at His wisdom (Matt. 22:15-22).

Noah

Noah had a revelation of things to come and was given the word of wisdom to know what to do and how to do it. As a result he possessed the supernatural ability to construct a huge boat on dry land that was sea worthy enough to weather the storms that came on the earth because of the flood. He was also given the insight and wisdom necessary to care for animals and people on an extended sea voyage.

Noah could have received the revelation about things to come and done nothing about it. The flood would have come just as God planned and Noah and his family would have perished. Noah, however, began to immediately work by faith on the wisdom God gave him to build an ark so that both his family and the animals would be safe. *"Thus did Noah; according to all that God commanded him, so did he"* (Genesis 6:22).

When a person receives a revelation, or a word of knowledge, from God, they must also await the further directions on what to do with that knowledge until a word of wisdom is received. When the word of wisdom has been received, it is time to fulfil their part of the plan.

God looks for those who are receptive to hearing His voice and are able and willing to carry His plan out faithfully. God never speaks just to hear Himself talk. He always has a direction and purpose.

Jehoshaphat

Jehoshaphat, king of Judah faced an impossible foe of invaders but he did not let fear dominate him. He dominated fear and turned himself over to God's direction. He declared a national fast so the people would all be in one accord with him as he waited for God's leadership. Meanwhile, he prayed and reminded God of His great power and might, that no one could stand against God, and that they were descendants of God's friend forever, Abraham. He said that they were limited and hopeless but knew that God was in control of their destiny.

As they were waiting on God for direction, the Spirit of the Lord came on one of the congregation named Jahaziel. Jahaziel spoke the word of God to them saying, *"Be not afraid nor dismayed by reason of this great multitude; for the battle is not yours, but God's."* He then went on to tell them the exact location of the enemy and the time they should go out against them to win the victory. *"Ye shall not need to fight in the battle; set yourselves, stand ye still, and see the salvation of the Lord with you, O Judah and Jerusalem: fear not, nor be dismayed; tomorrow go out against them for the Lord will be with you."*

After God's encouragement, they worshipped the Lord and believed His word for them to be true. The next morning, King Jehoshaphat admonished them again, *"Believe in the Lord your God, so shall ye be established; believe his prophets, so shall ye prosper."*

Then the King did his part and appointed singers to go before the army to praise the beauty of holiness as they went. *"And when they began to sing and to praise, the Lord set ambushments against the children of Ammon, Moab, and mount Seir, which were come against Judah; and they were smitten. And when Judah came toward the watch tower in the wilderness, they looked unto the multitude, and behold, they were dead bodies fallen to the earth, and none escaped"* (2 Chronicles 20:15,17, 20, 22).

God gave Jehoshaphat the divine wisdom to know that if the people were singing and praising God, they could not fear and doubt. It is impossible for the mind to think on two things simultaneously. Their minds were riveted in faith and expectation. They were waiting to see what God would do for them.

Joseph

God reveals a word of wisdom to people He plans to use, such as Joseph in Egypt when he saved that country from years of famine. God gave Joseph the interpretation of Pharaoh's dream and then gave him a word of wisdom about how he could save the people from starvation. Because of Joseph's faithfulness, the whole nation survived as well as Joseph's father and eleven brothers with their families.

Joseph's secret was he had learned that all divine wisdom comes from God. "*Do not interpretations belong to God?*" (Genesis 40:8).

Divine wisdom spoken at the right time is recognized as superior to human wisdom even by the ungodly. "*And Pharaoh said unto his servants, Can we find such a one as this is, a man in whom the spirit of God is? And Pharaoh said unto Joseph, Forasmuch as God hath showed thee all this, there is none so discreet and wise as thou art: Thou shalt be over my house, and according unto thy word shall all my people be ruled: only in the throne will I be greater than thou*" (Genesis 41:38-40).

Joseph did not force the wisdom of God on Pharaoh, he waited to be called and asked for his insight. "*When wisdom entereth into thine heart, and knowledge is pleasant unto thy soul; discretion shall preserve thee, understanding shall keep thee: to deliver thee from the way of the evil man, from the man that speaketh froward [perverse] things;*" (Proverbs 2:10-12).

Joseph the Step-father of Jesus

Joseph, the stepfather of Jesus, was warned by an angel in a dream about the events that were at hand. Herod had plans to kill all the babies in the environs of Jerusalem. Joseph was given the wisdom from God about how to avoid the dangers planned for his little family. He took the mother and child and went to Egypt where they would be safe until the Lord called them back again. In this way, God spared the seed that He had placed on the earth to fulfill His promise of salvation for all of mankind.

"*Behold, the angel of the Lord appeareth to Joseph in a dream, saying, Arise, and take the young child and his mother, and flee into Egypt, and be thou there until I bring thee word: for Herod will seek the young child to destroy him. When he arose, he took the young child and his mother by night, and departed into Egypt: And was there until the death of Herod: that it might be fulfilled which was spoken of the Lord by the prophet, saying, Out of Egypt have I called my son*" (Matthew 2:13-15).

THE GIFTS OF THE HOLY SPIRIT ARE FOR YOU!

Problem Solving Wisdom

In the early Church of Acts 6, we see that the wisdom of God was given to the disciples to choose out seven men of honest report, full of the Holy Ghost and wisdom to attend to the daily food distribution. This left the twelve disciples free to pray and minister the word. This discussion pleased the whole crowd, even the Grecians, whose widows felt neglected (Acts 6:1-7).

Paul

"...the Holy Ghost said, Separate me Barnabas and Saul for the work whereunto I have called them" (Acts 13:2).

"Long before, God had called Paul, informing him that he was a chosen messenger to the Gentiles. But the timing of God's will was not clear to Paul. A genuine word of wisdom (probably through prophecy) gave Paul his 'marching orders.' Please notice it was not a private, personal 'message.' It was a function of the Holy Spirit *in the Church*, exercised before Spirit-filled witnesses" (What You Should Know About the Holy Spirit, 1975, pp. 117, 118).

On another occasion Paul, the apostle, received a visitation from an angel in the midst of his crisis in a storm and was assured they would all be saved if they followed instructions. Paul gave those instructions to the captain and crew and as a result, they all survived. If they had tried to resolve the problem in their own strength, they would have perished at sea.

"And now I exhort you to be of good cheer: for there shall be no loss of any man's life among you, but of the ship. For there stood by me this night the angel of God, whose I am, and whom I serve, Saying, Fear not, Paul; thou must be brought before Caesar: and, lo, God hath given thee all them that sail with thee. Wherefore, sirs, be of good cheer: for I believe God, that it shall be even as it was told me. Howbeit we must be cast upon a certain island. And as the shipmen were about to flee out of the ship, when they had let down the boat into the sea, under color as though they would have cast anchors out of the foreship, Paul said to the centurion and to the soldiers, Except these abide in the ship, y cannot be saved. Then the soldiers cut off the ropes of the boat, and let her fall off. Wherefore I pray you to take some meat: for this is for your health: for there shall not a hair fall

from the head of any of you. And when they had eaten enough, they lightened the ship, and cast out the wheat into the sea. And when they had taken up the anchors, they committed themselves unto the sea, and loosed the rudder bands, and hoisted up the mainsail to the wind, and made toward shore . . . and so it came to pass, that they escaped all safe to land" (Acts 27:22-26, 30-32, 34, 38, 40, 44).

The gift of the word of wisdom is not for everyday guidance, it is usually for specific times of direction. It is distinguished from the ordinary by being extra ordinary wisdom about a situation, an insight from God, that only He could give us. Often times, a word of wisdom will change the course of history.

Jesus taught that the Holy Spirit would bring things to our remembrance and give us the right things to say when we're facing times of crisis. *"But the Comforter, which is the Holy Ghost, whom the Father will send in my name, he shall teach you all things, and bring all things to your remembrance, whatsoever I have said unto you"* (John 14:26).

When believers are confronted with people who would try to hinder or tear down the work of God, the Holy Spirit will give them divine wisdom. They will know what to speak and how to deal with the situation if the person is receptive to receive the word of wisdom.

A Word of Wisdom Spoken In the Night

Sometimes when a person is wrestling with a problem, the Lord will speak to them when they are resting quietly. *"Stand in awe, and sin not: commune with your own heart upon your bed, and be still. Selah. Offer the sacrifices of righteousness, and put your trust in the Lord. There be many that say, Who will show us any good? Lord, lift thou up the light of thy countenance upon us"* (Psalm 4:4-6).

"Commit thy works unto the Lord, and thy thoughts shall be established" (Proverbs 16:3).

The Test

How is the gift of the word of wisdom tested? Anyone could stand up and declare that they have a word of wisdom about a situation but how are people assured that it is from God? We're told to judge the gifts of the Spirit. *"Let the prophets speak two or three, and let the other judge"* (1 Corinthians 14:29).

God will always confirm His word if we ask Him to in the mouth of several witnesses. *"But if he will not hear thee, then take with thee one or two more, that in the mouth of two or three witnesses every word may be established."* (Matthew 18:16) *"This is the third time I am coming to you. In the mouth of two or three witnesses shall every word be established"* (2 Corinthians 13:1).

Another primary way of receiving confirmation is through the written Word of God. A gift of the word of wisdom will never contradict the written Word of God.

The gift of the word of wisdom, as with anything God wants to speak to us about, should always bear witness in the spirit of the believer. *"For as many as are led by the Spirit of God, they are the sons of God. The Spirit itself beareth witness with our spirit, that we are the children of God"* (Romans 8:14,16).

The Word of Wisdom Is For All

According to the weight of scripture, the word of wisdom was given for all believers to profit. Each believer needs God's words of wisdom to guide them along life's pathway. Paul understood the necessity of this wisdom when he spoke and preached the word. He tried to explain to the Corinthian church that the anointing on his words was from the Holy Spirit giving words of wisdom and knowledge as he spoke.

"And my speech and my preaching was not with enticing words of man's wisdom, but in demonstration of the Spirit and of power: That your faith should not stand in the wisdom of men, but in the power of God. Howbeit we speak wisdom among them that are perfect: yet not the wisdom of this world, nor of the princes of this world, that come to nought: But we speak the wisdom of God in a mystery, even the hidden wisdom, which God ordained before the world unto our glory: Which none of the princes of this world knew: for had they known it, they would not have crucified the Lord of glory.

"But God hath revealed them unto us by his Spirit: for the Spirit searcheth all things, yea, the deep things of God. For what Man knoweth the things of a man save the spirit of man which is in him? even so the things of God knoweth no man, but the Spirit of God.

84

Now we have received not the spirit of the world, but the spirit which is of God: that we might know the things that are freely given to us of God. But the natural man receiveth not the things of the Spirit of God: for they are foolishness unto him: neither can he know them, because they are spiritually discerned. For who hath known the mind of the Lord, that he may instruct him? But we have the mind of Christ.” (1 Corinthians 2: 4-8, 10-12, 14, 16).

According to this, Paul explains that it is the Holy Spirit that knows the deep things of God and breaks them down so we can understand them through the revelation of a word of wisdom or knowledge. People who receive revelations of God can share them with others by framing them in their own words. They do not loose their power because they are put into understandable words for the listeners. They retain the power of God in them because they have come from His divine inspiration and anointing.

Because the Word of Wisdom is unconstrained by natural education or experience, it may be revealed to children such as Samuel, a slave like Joseph, or a brilliant statesman like Daniel.

What Is The Focus of This Wisdom?

“But of him are ye in Christ Jesus, who of God is made unto us wisdom, and righteousness, and sanctification, and redemption: ’ (1 Corinthians 1:30).

God's wisdom—salvation and sanctification through a crucified Christ—has been ‘hidden’ in a ‘mystery’ (2:7). His wise plan of redemption is secret or mysterious in the sense that it was hidden in God from all human eyes but is now manifested in Christ and revealed through the Spirit (2:7-10) Yet God's wisdom still remains hidden to those who consider the message of the cross ‘foolishness’ (1:18; 2:14).

“The primary and authoritative revelation of God's secret wisdom was given to Paul (4:1) and to the other apostles and prophets (Ephesians 3:3-6). But according to 1 Corinthians 12:8, insight into this divine wisdom, when spoken forth, is a spiritual gift available to the entire body of Christ” (Words of Wisdom & Knowledge, Charisma Mag. Nov. 1992).

The wisdom that is given and spoken out is a divine wisdom

that supersedes the capacity and experiences of the one speaking.

A genuine word of wisdom, although it speaks profoundly, will never add or subtract anything from scripture. Scripture will always be the primary source of wisdom and knowledge from God.

It has been said that, "wisdom builds with the material which knowledge provides. Wisdom is knowledge in action" (The Spirit Himself, 1949, p. 127).

"The gift of the word of wisdom is a supernatural revealing to an individual of the will and purpose of God. In other words, it reveals either what God is doing, what He is planning to do or what He wants done.

"This word of wisdom may simply reveal to you God's purpose, or it may specifically show you an action to take regarding a situation" (Who's Afraid of the Holy Ghost?, 1994, p. 131).

The key to walking in the gift of the word of wisdom is found in one's relationship to Christ. *"In whom are hid all the treasures of wisdom and knowledge"* (Colossians 2:3).

CHAPTER 10

THE GIFT OF DISCERNING OF SPIRITS

The gift of Discerning of Spirits is the supernatural ability to separate between what is from the spiritual area in contrast to the human or soulish areas. It is also able to differentiate between good and evil spirits.

To "discern" means to perceive, distinguish or differentiate. This gift gives insight into the spiritual realm. It is given mainly for the purpose of deliverance from demons, revealing servants of Satan, exposing and defeating works or expressions of demons, and exposing error. Donald Gee describes the operation of this gift as "a piercing of all that is merely outward, and seeing right through; then forming a judgment based on that insight" (Concerning Spiritual Gifts, 1937, p. 51).

There are three basic spirit sources: the Holy Spirit, the demonic spirits, and the human spirit. On occasion, believers need to be able to detect the origin of a spirit to one of these groupings.

"Even though we tend to be unconscious of the spirit world surrounding us, we are really highly influenced and controlled by it. Sinners are said to be taken captive by the devil and are controlled by his will in the spirit realm. (2 Timothy 2:26) This is not something weird or unusual, rather it is the way things have been since shortly after Adam was created" (The Holy Spirit Today, A concise survey of the doctrine of the Holy Ghost, 1976, p.75).

Satan's counterfeit of this gift of discerning of spirits is his use of a lying spirit or a spirit of divination. He always has a counterfeit for God's genuine gifts.

THE GIFTS OF THE HOLY SPIRIT ARE FOR YOU!

In scripture there are many accounts of people seeing angels and Satan with their natural eyes. Eve encountered the devil as he appeared as a serpent to her. David was provoked by Satan to number Israel (1 Chronicles 2:11). The High Priest, Joshua, while he was serving the Lord in the temple had Satan appear to him (Zechariah 3:1). Jesus saw and talked to the devil. There are seven times when different ones encountered Satan face to face in scripture.

There are many events and times when it is documented that persons encountered or saw angelic beings. Adam and Eve saw cherubim and a flaming sword set at the entrance to the garden when they left the Garden of Eden (Genesis 3:24). An angel appeared and helped Hagar in the desert (Genesis 16:7). An angel appeared to the parents of Samson (Judges 13:21), also to Gideon (Judges 6:12), calling them to lead the Israelites to victory over their enemies. In the New Testament are recorded various times when angels intervened in the affairs of men also. An angel appeared to Mary (Luke 1:28), and Joseph (Matthew 2:13-15), before Christ was born and afterwards to help them escape danger. An angel was at the tomb and spoke to the women when they came to see Jesus (Matthew 27:2). They appeared to Peter (Acts 12:7), and Paul (Acts 27), in times of danger to lead them out of prison and through a storm.

"God is surrounded by spirit beings in the heavenlies. We read about angels, seraphim and cherubim, all of which are spiritual beings. (Hebrews 1:7, 14; Genesis 3:24; Isaiah 6:2-6) We are also told that there are incalculable numbers of them. (Daniel 7:10; Matthew 26:53) God is called the 'Lord of Hosts'" (Ibid, 1976, p. 75).

There are other accounts in scripture where it is mentioned that an evil spirit was present and no one saw anything with the natural eye, but discerned it by the power of the Holy Spirit.

Paul in Acts 16:16-18, knew by the gift of discerning of spirits that a spirit of divination was possessing and working in a young girl who had been following him and Silas. He rebuked the spirit of divination and commanded it to come out of her and it left that same hour. She had been sent there by Satan to confuse and cause problems in that new congregation of believers.

There is a need to be more sensitive to the warning that the gift of discerning of spirits can give about satanic attacks against our bodies, the church, our families, etc.

Man's spirit can be carnal and rise up against what the purpose and direction of God is. We need to know what we're dealing with spiritually. This comes by understanding the purpose and functions of this gift. Paul talked about the last days being perilous days in 2 Timothy, when deception would be rampant. "New-agers" and people involved in the occult are infiltrating churches and causing chaos with an increasing frequency and trying to divide the body of Christ.

The gift of discerning of spirits will warn people of danger and expose people who are being controlled by unclean spirits.

How Do We Recognize This Gift Is at Work?

Norval Hayes says, "Your spirit will become grieved. That's God's number one way to show you somebody else's spirit: when you're around them, your spirit becomes grieved. You will not feel *right* about the person" (The Gift of Discerning of Spirits, 1979, p. 40).

The gift of discerning of spirits will sometimes cause a discomfort or disturbance in a believer's spirit area, making them aware of the Holy Spirit's warning system about something they are seeing, hearing or reading. It causes them to know that what they are involved in is in conflict with God's Spirit and the Word of God. When that happens, it is their obligation to study the scriptures and find out what the conflict is so it can be corrected before it causes any confusion and division.

I Corinthians 14:33 says, *"For God is not the author of confusion, but of peace, as in all churches of the saints."* If anything is creating confusion or chaos, questions need to be asked. People need to seek the face of God to find out why His Holy Spirit is warning them and what needs to be done about it.

James 1:5 instructs us: *"If any of you lack wisdom, let him ask of God, that giveth to all men liberally, and upbraideth not; and it shall be given him."*

The Holy Spirit will guide each person to the scriptures and show them if there is something wrong going on and how to correct it. Scripture corrects, teaches proper doctrine, and is a discerner of things. *"For the word of God is quick and powerful, and sharper than any two edged sword, piercing even to the dividing asunder of soul and spirit, and of the joints and marrow, and is a discerner of the thoughts and intents of the heart.*"

Discerning of spirits may come to a person through a vision during a time of ministry or prayer. The vision can open up a view into the spirit world, showing a circumstance or problem that needs to be taken care of in a precise way as the Holy Spirit instructs.

The gift of discerning of spirits may be checked by two biblical tests: the doctrinal (1 John 4:1-6) and the practical (Matthew 7:15-23).

"The New Testament clearly teaches that every Christian needs to be able to tell good from evil, right from wrong. Hebrews 5:14 says mature Christians 'have their senses exercised to discern both good and evil.' The Berean Christians were commended for not being naive. They tested the preaching of the apostles against Scripture as we all must (see Acts 17:11). First John 4:1 is explicit in telling us to 'not believe every spirit, but test the spirits whether they are of God'" (Your Spiritual Gifts, Can Help Your Church Grow, 1982, p. 96).

Discerning of Spirits for Healing

Discerning of spirits reveals when an evil spirit needs to be bound to accomplish healing in a person. A spirit of fear, infirmity, dumb and deaf spirit, etc. can block a person from receiving their healing. If the person has given a foothold to the enemy to hassle them, they need to shut the door and regain control over that area of the flesh.

In Matthew 9:33, Jesus looked behind the physical dumb and deafness and all the other symptoms that manifested in the young man and recognized the demon causing the problem. He cast the demon out and healed the young man as the crowd looked on in amazement. Casting out the demon played a major part in this story of the boy's healing.

God's Word provides the various names of strongman spirits that want to attack and neutralize people spiritually and physically. Their names are mentioned in scripture so there is no need to fabricate new ones. If God's Word calls a spirit by a specific name we can be sure it exists. The Word of God also defines each one's capabilities and diabolical specialties. (See other books on this subject by Dr. Carol Robeson, ie. "Strongman's His Name, What's His Game?" and "Strongman's His Name II"; Whittaker House, Inc.)

When encountered, the evil spirits need to be bound and rebuked in the name of Jesus to accomplish any work that needs to be done. The Holy Spirit can confirm to our spirit which unclean spirits are the right ones to bind in the Name of Jesus as He commanded. *"Or else how can one enter into a strong man's house, and spoil his goods, except he first binds the strong man? and then he will spoil his house (Matthew 12:29)." "Behold, I give unto you power to tread on serpents and scorpions, and over all the power of the enemy: and nothing shall by any means harm you (Luke 10:19)."*

After binding the unclean spirit, the believer can release the healing virtue or power given as a gift of the Holy Spirit to work for him without any further hindrance.

The gift of the word of knowledge or the gift of the word of wisdom and prophecy often work with the gift of discerning of spirits.

How Do We Discern Spirits?

In 1 John 4:1, we're told, *"Beloved, do not believe every spirit, but test the spirits, whether they are of God, because many false prophets have gone out into the world."*

How do we prove a spirit? By asking the Holy Spirit to reveal what the source of the activity in question is. He uses the knowledge we have of God's Word to bring to remembrance things that will either confirm God's presence or reveal any demonic or human sources. Each person is responsible for being current in their walk with the Lord always so when the need arises, the Holy Spirit can bear witness with their spirit about a given matter and thus confirm one way or the other what is being asked about.

"For as many as are led by the Spirit of God, these are sons of God. The Spirit Himself bears witness with our spirit that we are children of God" (Romans 8:14,16).

"Notice, it is never *us* attempting to gain a contact; rather it is God breaking in on the privacy of our world to supply us with information we need. Normally these contacts from God will take us by surprise. *Our task is to be in a position to hear God's voice.* This is one major part of prayer, and a definite result of the Work working in our lives" (Seducing Spirits and Doctrines of Demons, 1988, p. 137).

In John, chapters 14 to 16, Jesus spent much time talking about the benefits of the Holy Spirit. One of those benefits he mentioned specifically was that the Holy Spirit would be a guide to all truth.

This certifies that believers do not need to talk to or interview unholy spirits to gain truth or guidance. Nor is it proper to believe a person can get any factual information from lying demonic entities. It is the Holy Spirit who will reveal truth, not an unholy spirit.

"Much of the occult today exists on the assumption that everything that is supernatural is divine and therefore part of valid religion. But this assumption is erroneous" (What You Should Know About the Holy Spirit, 1975, p. 118).

"But the Comforter, which is the Holy Ghost, whom the Father will send in my name, he shall teach you all things, and bring all things to your remembrance, whatsoever I have said unto you" (John 14:26). "Howbeit when he, the Spirit of truth is come, he will guide you into all truth: for he shall not speak of himself; but whatsoever he shall hear, that shall he speak: and he will show you things to come. He shall glorify me: for he shall receive of mine, and shall show it unto you" (John 16:13,14).

In spite of this teaching by Jesus Himself, ignorant or unlearned Christians still insist on asking questions of lying demons who do their best to deceive people at every turn. If the devil will lie, so will his minions and the demons under his control. *"Ye are of your father the devil, and the lusts of your father ye will do. He was a murderer from the beginning, and abode not in the truth, because there is no truth in him. When he speaketh a lie, he speaketh of his own: for he is a liar, and the father of it" (John 8:44).*

The gift of discerning of spirits is God's provision to us when it comes to dealing with the devil and his demons. Believers have the Word of God and the witness of the Holy Spirit, they do not need to sit around making useless conversation with lying demons. When a person discovers that someone is a liar, usually it invalidates anything they say. We know that the devil is a liar and it therefore discredits anything he or his underlings would say. They cannot be trusted. Christians should be seeking the guidance and wisdom of the Holy Spirit, not unholy spirits.

When confronted with demonic activity, the person needs to be asked where a door was opened to allow this type of turmoil. The door to that or any other work of the flesh must be closed by confession and repentance with a new resolve not to indulge in the works of the flesh again. *"Now the works of the flesh are manifest, which are these; adultery, fornication, uncleanness, lasciviousness, Idolatry, witchcraft, hatred, variance, emulations, wrath, strife, seditions, heresies, Envyings, murders, drunkenness, revellings, and such like: of the which I tell you before, as I have also told you in time past, that they which do such things shall not inherit the kingdom of God"* (Galatians 5:19-21).

The Three-fold Warning System

A smoke alarm goes off whenever it senses there is something burning. It is ready day or night and will react to anything that gives off an undue amount of smoke.

A believer's three-fold warning system is better than the best smoke alarm. The Word of God is first, then an inner witness of the Holy Spirit, followed by the gift of discerning of spirits given by the Holy Spirit who lives in each believer.

The secret to being more accurate with these tools, is for the believer to learn to fine-tune himself to the leading of God's Spirit and recognize when He is trying to warn of some impending danger or deception.

The gift of discerning of spirits is not a natural intuition or suspicion. It is not mind-reading or E.S.P. It is not permission to judge another person with one's own intellect.

"Judge not, that ye be not judged, For with what judgment ye judge, ye shall be judged: and with what measure ye mete, it shall be measured to you again." (Matthew 7:1,2).

In the context of Matthew 7:15-20, we are told to judge the fruit of a person's life and in 1 John 4:1, we are told to judge the spirits to see whether they are from God or not.

Satan can, and will, try to appear as an angel of light, bringing seemingly good things to people. He will use carnal people to even pose as apostles and ministers to deceive any that he can. *"For such are false apostles, deceitful workers, transforming themselves into the apostles of Christ. And no marvel; for Satan himself is transformed into an angel of light. Therefore it is no great thing if his ministers also be transformed as the ministers of righteousness; whose end shall be according to their work"* (2 Corinthians 11:13-15).

Believers must always be careful not to be overcome by how beautiful or handsome a personality looks. Satan will use even this to deceive some who are interested in the cosmetics of things. Satan was a beautifully created being before he was thrown out of heaven. *"Thine heart was lifted up because of thy beauty, thou hast corrupted thy wisdom by reason of thy brightness: I will cast thee to the ground, I will lay thee before kings, that they may behold thee"* (Ezekiel 28:17).

Lucifer, as he was known then, lost his beauty when sin was revealed in him and he chose to become the adversary or deceiver, better known as Satan. He knows the value of presenting his deception through vehicles that have an appearance of beauty. He used what he had to deceive one third of the angels and took them with him to their sure destruction.

A believer must not let any evil dazzle or fascinate them to the point of playing with it mentally or outwardly for even a second of time. Sometimes the enemy will approach believers with the idea that they can rescue someone who is in sin, only to deceive them and wear them out with lies and betrayal. Everything must be weighed by the balance of the Word of God.

Spirits Have Names

There are sixteen spirits, or strongmen, mentioned by name in the Bible that we should be aware of enough to recognize them by their evil fruit and actions. When a believer is knowledgeable of an unclean spirit through the gift of discerning of spirits he does not need to be fearful. He has been given all the power and authority necessary to bind him and get rid of his activities (Luke 10:19).

A listing of these spirits mentioned by name in the Bible are as follows: (Strongman's His Name, What's His Game?, 1983).

1. The familiar spirit - 1 Samuel 28
2. The spirit of divination - Acts 16:16

3. The spirit of jealousy - Numbers 5:14
4. A lying spirit -2 Chronicles 18:22
5. A perverse spirit - Isaiah 19:14
6. A spirit of haughtiness - Proverbs 16:18
7. A spirit of heaviness - Isaiah 61:3
8. A spirit of whoredoms - Hosea 4:12
9. A spirit of infirmity - Luke 13:11
10. Dumb and deaf spirit - Mark 9:25
11. Spirit of bondage - Romans 8:15
12. Spirit of fear - 2 Timothy 1:7
13. Seducing Spirits - 2 Timothy 4:1
14. Spirit of anti-christ - 1 John 4:3
15. Spirit of error - 1 John 4:6
16. Spirit of death - Revelation 9:11; 20:13,14

These strongmen are also recognized by the fruit they produce in a situation or in a person's life. They always leave an identifiable trail of their activities.

The gift of discerning of spirits reveals the servants of Satan. *"Then Saul, (who also is called Paul,) filled with the Holy Ghost, set his eyes on him, And said, O full of all subtilty and all mischief, thou child of the devil, thou enemy of all righteousness, wilt thou not cease to pervert the right ways of the Lord?" (Acts 13:9,10)*

The gift of discerning of spirits reveals the truth from a lie. It exposes the intentions of the devil in situations. The Holy Spirit unmasks and levels the devil.

The Holy Spirit will expose a lie even when it is very carefully devised and sounds like the truth. He is like a spiritual police officer who arrests the unjust and sets a guard over the innocent. He sees to it that there is warning of any troublemakers who would try to destroy the body of Christ.

Prophecies

The gift of discerning of spirits will help believers know when a word from God is false and not from God at all. It is a safeguard that the Holy Spirit has given the body of Christ to protect it from false teachers and prophets that would try to sneak in undetected and deceive a whole group.

THE GIFTS OF THE HOLY SPIRIT ARE FOR YOU!

All the gifts of the Spirit are 100% pure, but the vessels God has to use are at varying degrees of cleanness or sanctification. For example, a word of God spoken to His people is totally pure but when a person receives the thought or word from God, they may frame that word using some of their own thoughts and in the process tarnish it. Consequently, we are told to judge prophecies, etc. and hold fast to that part that is good. Even as youngsters we are taught physically to eat the meat and be careful not to swallow any bones, we must learn to do this spiritually also.

Satan attempts to counterfeit the divine works of God by producing an external appearance that is appealing and similar to the work of the Holy Spirit. The gift of discerning of spirits empowers a Christian to ascertain the source of true gifts and messages from God.

God Is Not Out Numbered

God's heavenly hosts are not outnumbered by the evil forces of Satan. One third of the angels followed Satan and became his minions but the other two-thirds are ready at a second's notice to be at the service of the believer. *"Are they not all ministering spirits, sent forth to minister for them who shall be heirs of salvation?" (Hebrews 1:14)*

Believers are commanded not to pray to angels, but can ask God to send out His emissaries to help when there is a need. Their work is specifically to minister to Christians during their spiritual journey here on earth. The heavenly hosts of angels are careful to give glory and honor to God always.

The gift of discerning of spirits should make believers aware of angelic beings and their intervention in lives. The angels minister strength and shield the believer from many attacks of the enemy spirits. Many Biblical figures were aware of God's angelic presence helping them. John on the Isle of Patmos saw the angels involved in all the different aspects of things to come and also at the present time.

The gift of discerning of spirits should cause one to know immediately when the voice of God is speaking. When the voice of God spoke to young Samuel, the old priest, Eli, knew it was God and instructed Samuel to listen. The prophets of old heard the voice of

God and spoke it forth with power. They also knew the voice of the false prophet was not a message from God because it did not measure up to God's divine character.

Walking in Faith

Every believer is commanded to walk by faith and live in the spirit, not in the flesh. When this is being done, he can resist the devil and scripture declares that the devil flees from him in James 4:7. In 1 John 4:4 we're told, "Greater is He that is in you than he that is in the world." If a Christian is living correctly, with a current relationship with Christ, the promise of 1 John 5:18 applies to him also. *"We know that whosoever is born of God sinneth not; but he that is begotten of God keepeth himself, and that wicked one toucheth him not."*

This final verse declares that if a person is serving God, the devil cannot touch him. The Greek says, *"Cannot attach himself"* to a person.

"But if the Spirit of him that raised up Jesus from the dead dwell in you, he that raised up Christ from the dead shall also quicken your mortal bodies by his Spirit that dwelleth in you." Romans 8:11

Diagram 11:1

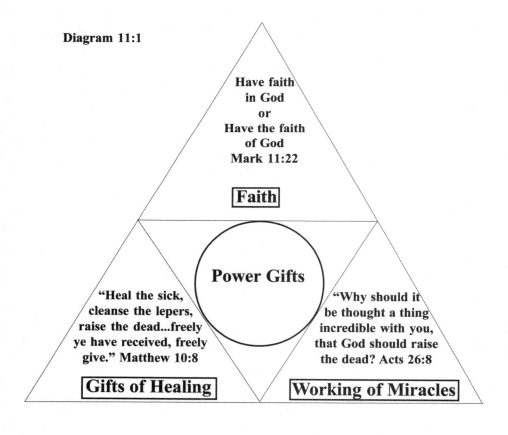

Have faith in God or Have the faith of God Mark 11:22

Faith

Power Gifts

"Heal the sick, cleanse the lepers, raise the dead...freely ye have received, freely give." Matthew 10:8

"Why should it be thought a thing incredible with you, that God should raise the dead? Acts 26:8

Gifts of Healing

Working of Miracles

"According as his divine power hath given unto us all things that pertain unto life and godliness." 2 Peter 3:1

CHAPTER 11

THE GIFTS OF HEALINGS

In this third group of spiritual gifts we find the power gifts. Healing becomes evident throughout scripture as the most widely distributed of the power gifts. The gifts of healings are for the supernatural healing of diseases and infirmities. These can take the form of healing in the spirit, soul or body areas. These gifts supernaturally do what no physician or psychologist can do with all their years of training.

Jesus used this gift on numerous occasions during his lifetime and gave his disciples the same authority over disease. *"Heal the sick, cleanse the lepers, raise the dead, cast out devils; freely ye have received, freely give"* (Matthew 10:8).

This gift is the one that lifted common fishermen, etc. into prominence in the early church while unregenerate men enviously desired the secret of their success.

The devil fights the healing ministry with fervor because it is such a tangible thing. People can see it. It has an especially potent witness in a physical world.

Again, it is emphasized, the character of this gift is entirely supernatural. Healings are given by the power of Christ through the anointing of the Holy Spirit on common people who may be completely ignorant of any natural medical knowledge. This is a gift that is always given away to someone else in need. The person praying is just the conductor through which the gift passes to the one who is healed. They are like a wire that conducts electricity from an electrical outlet to a light bulb. They're connected to the Power Source. No one person possesses a gift of healing. It is the Holy Spirit who bestows them as He sees the need.

The Greek rendering of the word *healing* is as follows: healing, (the termination denoting the complete act; the result or product of the act) and also, (the termination denoting the complete act; the result or product of the act,) (A Critical Lexicon and Concordance To The English and Greek New Testament, 1979, p. 360).

It should be noted that the title of this gift is a double plural. God has as many methods of healing people as there are needs. "Used in the phrase *charismata iamáton*, (*charismata* the pl. of *chárisma* [5486], gift; *iamáton*, gen., of healings), gifts of healings. It is always in the pl. (1 Cor. 12:9, 28, 30). The Lord did not give *iámata*, which would be certain drugs for healing, but only gifts or abilities to provide the means of various healings in His divine providence, whether they be with or without medicine" (The Complete Word Study Dictionary, New Testament, 1993, p. 752).

Healing was provided for in the Old Testament and confirmed in the New Testament by Jesus as being the will of God. *"How God anointed Jesus of Nazareth with the Holy Ghost and with power: who went about doing good, and healing all that were oppressed of the devil; for God was with him" (Acts 10:38).*

Jesus gave the promise of healing to each believer. *"They shall take up serpents; and if they drink any deadly thing, it shall not hurt them; they shall lay hands on the sick, and they shall recover" (Mark 16:18).*

Healing was also given as a gift of the Holy Spirit. *"To another faith by the same Spirit; to another the gifts of healing by the same Spirit;" (1 Cor 12:9).* "The 'gifts of healings' are the most frequently performed of the gifts of power . . . The gifts of healings, since they are the gifts of the Holy Ghost, are divine enablements to heal the sick apart from the aid of natural means and human skill . . . This power of Christ to heal is transferred and conveyed to Spirit-filled believers in and through the 'gifts of healings'" (The Spirit Himself, 1949, pp. 139-140).

Isaiah 53:4,5 prophesied that Jesus would carry our sicknesses and heal our infirmities. *"Surely he hath borne our griefs, and carried our sorrows: yet we did esteem him stricken, smitten of God, and afflicted. But he was wounded for our transgressions, he was bruised for our iniquities: the chastisement of our peace was upon him; and with his stripes we are healed."*

James 5:14,15 instructs people to anoint and pray for the sick. *"Is any sick among you? let him call for the elders of the church; and let them pray over him, anointing him with oil in the name of the Lord: And the prayer of faith shall save the sick, and the Lord shall raise him up; and if he have committed sins, they shall be forgiven him."*

First Peter shows healing as an accomplished fact and ties it into the atonement by noting that healing was procured by Jesus' stripes. *"Who his own self bare our sins in his own body on the tree, that we, being dead to sins, should live unto righteousness: by whose stripes ye were healed"* (I Peter 2:24,25).

"There is something higher even than the Cross. It is the Resurrection of our Lord. There the Gospel of Healing finds the fountain of its deepest life. The death of Christ destroys sin—The root of sickness. But it is the life of Jesus which supplies the source of health and life for our redeemed bodies. The body of Christ is the living fountain of all our vital strength" (The Gospel of Healing, 1915, p. 35).

It is the name, nature and work of God to heal because He is Life. He said in Exodus 15:26, *"I am the Lord [Jehovah-Ropheka], that healeth thee."* and in Ps 103:3, *"who healeth all thine diseases."*

Healing is a powerful testimony to the divine power of God in action. Healing speaks loudly to a world of unbelieving spectators when they see an incurable disease or ailment healed. Nearly everyone has something that needs medical attention. When they realize that God actually is interested in people's lives to the point that He has personally reached down and provided healing they immediately want to know more about Him. Many have accepted Jesus as their Savior after hearing about or seeing a healing of someone they knew.

Healing is part of the inheritance of the believer. Jesus died and left a legacy of healing. Therefore, it is ours to enjoy. No one needs to shrink away from asking God for His healing provision. *"For we have not a high priest which cannot be touched with the feeling of our infirmities; but was in all points tempted like as we are, yet with-*

out sin. Let us therefore come boldly unto the throne of grace, that we may obtain mercy, and find grace to help in time of need" (Heb. 4:15,16).

There is no greater time of need in a person's life than when they feel pain or have an incurable sickness. Only God can remove disease and pain permanently.

"For this purpose the Son of God was manifested, that he might destroy the works of the devil" (1 John 3:8). Medicine tries to mask pain with pain killers as it combats infections and diseases with drugs. God has provided the knowledge to discover the drugs for the healing of the body. Surgeons perform surgery and cut out diseases parts of the body, but only God can heal the wound and complete the process of healing.

"The gift of healing does not make doctors and nurses obsolete. In many cases, God is pleased to use modern medical means of healing, although this should not be confused with the gift of healing" (Your Spiritual Gifts Can Help Your Church Grow, 1994, p. 211).

Sickness is a work of the devil that was destroyed. Sickness and disease entered the world when sin entered in the Garden of Eden. It brought the seeds of death with it. The end of all sickness is death if it is not somehow interrupted. To receive healing, believers need to have faith in the Lord's Word and in the gifts of healing and in the Lord Himself. Therefore it is vital that each believer renew his mind with the Word of God and establish a walk in the Spirit that leads us into a real worship of our Lord.

Then we need to hear the Word consistently, because faith (for healing) comes from hearing the Word of God. *"And be not conformed to this world: but be ye transformed by the renewing of your mind, that ye may prove what is that good, and acceptable, and perfect will of God"* (Romans 12:2).

Renewing the mind can only be possible by washing it with the water of the Word of God. A person's mind will be conformed to whatever it is receiving on a regular basis. If it is being fed junk food from some soap opera or rock music lyrics, that is what will determine the spiritual understanding a person has.

We are renewed in knowledge of God's Word. Knowledge comes by learning God's Word. The prescribed way of learning God's Word is by taking time to study it for yourself.

How the Gifts of Healings Operate

Usually the gifts of healing operate by a touch or a word. An exception would be when the shadow of Peter fell upon people and they were healed. However even that type of healing requires faith by the receiver for it to happen.

"Insomuch that they brought forth the sick into the streets, and laid them on beds and couches, that at the least the shadow of Peter passing by might overshadow some of them" (Acts 5:15).

Anointing with oil accompanying the prayers of the elders of the church as they lay hands on the sick will initiate healing (James 5:14-15).

God isn't boring, He is a God of great variety when it comes to the ways He chooses to heal people. Every time people think they have the formula, He changes the formula. God will not be stereotyped, He will be as original as He wants to be in a person's life. He wants to teach people to walk in daily obedience to His Word and Will.

In Jesus' ministry, He sometimes touched the sick. *"And Jesus, moved with compassion, put forth his hand, and touched him, and saith unto him, I will; be thou clean" (Mark 1:41). "And he cometh to Bethsaida; and they bring a blind man unto him, and besought him to touch him" (Mark 8:22).*

Jesus took the hand of the sick and at other times He put his hands on them. He saw the faith that was registering in their face as they heard the teaching and required an action to be completed. There were also people who came to him and touched Him or the hem of His garment. The woman with a flow of blood pushed through the crowd until she touched the hem of His garment for her healing.

Every believer, just like the disciples of Jesus, has been commanded to heal the sick. It will not be done in the same manner every time. The Holy Spirit will prompt a person how to approach each problem in the correct way. If a demon is causing the illness or infirmity, it must be stopped so that the body can be healed. It is the Holy Spirit that will enable a person to know exactly what approach to take." *Being confident of this very thing, that he which hath begun a good work in you will perform it until the day of Jesus Christ:" (Phil. 1:6). "But he answered and said, It is written, Man shall not live by bread alone, but by every word that proceedeth out of the mouth of God" (Mat. 4:4).*

We walk on the word of God. The part of the believer is to believe and trust God's Word without any hesitation or doubt. God's will give the proper understanding to the asker, seeker and believer on how to attain healing. *"He sent his word, and healed them, and delivered them from their destructions" (Psa. 107:20).*

The problem is that not enough people hear His Word, get it down in their spirit and work on it. Remember the parable of the sower. The birds came and ate up the seed which was the Word as soon as it was sown. Believers must hold on to the Word as it is preached and stop thinking about other things. The Word of God must penetrate its roots down under the surface, deep into the area of an individual's spirit for it to bring forth the thirty, sixty and hundred fold return that has been promised. It is the Word of God that bears the seed and will germinate and bring the evidence of healing.

Four Main Weapons

There are four main weapons available to each believer, according to scripture: The word of God, the Name of Jesus, the blood of Jesus and the word of our testimony. These are to be used on a daily basis.

Christians must never become discouraged when they are anointed by the Spirit to pray for someone and then not see an instantaneous manifestation. Healing takes place when the prayer is offered and the person walks by faith until they come into total agreement with the anointing, then the manifestation of healing takes place. "It is not a special gift of discriminating favoritism, but a great and common heritage of faith and obedience. It is 'Whosoever will let him take the water of life freely.' It is true that all who come must conform to the simple conditions of obedient faith; but these are impartial, without respect of persons, and within the reach of all who trust and obey" (The Gospel of Healing, 1915, p. 42).

If Jesus purchased healing for us in His redemption, it is God's will for us to have it. Christ's whole saving work at Calvary was the direct fulfilment of the God's will.

Because of doubt, many people throw the answer out the window. James 1: 6 says not to waver. An abiding faith in what the Word says is taking place, in spite of what is seen with the natural eye. There has to be a mind-set, based on God's Word and promises when anything is requested from God. *But let him ask in faith, nothing wavering. For he that wavereth is like a wave of the sea driven with the wind and tossed"* (James 1:6). *"If ye abide in me, and my words abide in you, ye shall ask what ye will, and it shall be done unto you"* (John 15:7).

Harold Horton listed some uses of the gifts of healings in the Scriptures.

    (a) First of all they are to deliver the sick and destroy the works of the devil in the human body (Acts 10:38).

    (b) To establish Jesus' astonishing claims (John 10:36-38).

    (c) To authorize the gospel message as preached by God's servants (Acts 4:29,30, 33,v:12) (Acts 7:6,7).

    (d) To establish the Resurrection of Jesus (Acts 3:15,16).

    (e) To draw people within the sound of the gospel (John 6:2).

    (f) To turn people to God.

    (g) To convince unbelievers of God's Word, mysterious though it may be.

    (h) To bring glory to God. Hallelujah! (Mark 2:12; Luke 13:17).

    (i) To inspire faith and courage in God's people (The Gifts of the Spirit, 1946, pp. 111-115).

THE GIFTS OF THE HOLY SPIRIT ARE FOR YOU!

CHAPTER 12

THE GIFT OF WORKING OF MIRACLES

Miracles are woven throughout the total fabric of the Bible. God's Word begins in Genesis 1:1 with the miracle of creation. From that point on miracles become a part of the Bible with promises of continuing miracles for today. All three persons of the God-head are given credit and glory for miracles.

"Then all the multitude kept silence, and gave audience to Barnabas and Paul, declaring what miracles and wonders God had wrought among the Gentiles by them" (Acts 15:12).

Jesus said, *"Verily, verily, I say unto you, He that believeth on me, the works that I do shall he do also; and greater works than these shall he do; because I go unto my Father"* (John 14:12). Scripture clearly declares believers are to ask and believe for things that are beyond the natural daily routine. Jesus did the supernatural and declared that this should become the normal activity of all believers.

The source of the gift of working of miracles today in the body of Christ is the Holy Spirit that indwells each believer. He is in complete agreement with God the Father and Jesus our Lord whenever a miracle is worked. *"Now there are diversities of gifts, but the same Spirit, And there are differences of administrations, but the same Lord. And there are diversites of operations, but it is the same God which worketh all in all"* (1 Corinthians 12: 4-6).**Described**

"To another the working of miracles; to another prophecy; to another . . . " (1 Corinthians 12:10).

Thomas Aquinas called the gift of working of miracles "the

107

winged sandals and the staff of the messengers."

Workings of Miracles are actually two plural Greek nouns meaning "energies, acts" and "potency or powers," the gift could be literally translated "working of powers" or "operations of works of powers." The word *dunamis*, which is translated *miracles* in 1 Corinthians 12:10, is the same word that is translated *power* in Acts 1:8 and Luke 24:49 and refers to Christ as the power in 1 Cor. 2: 24. This power was realized at the outpouring of the Spirit as prophesied in Acts 1:8, *"But ye shall receive power, after that the Holy Ghost is come upon you: and ye shall be witnesses unto me both in Jerusalem, and in all Judea, and in Samaria, and unto the uttermost part of the earth."*

"At Pentecost, the disciples received *dynamis*, meaning potency: That type of power is a latent force waiting to be drawn upon. When the need arises and we act in faith, that "dynamis" potential explodes into energy. It is like turning the key in the ignition of your car: The unseen power in your battery becomes electrical energy that surges into your starter motor, and your engine turns. That is not an impulse; it is a propulsion.

"Translators use the word 'miracle' to describe this manifestation of the 'workings of powers.' That word 'miracle' actually comes from a Latin term used to describe fairy-tale magic in the Greek and Roman myths. But the 'workings of powers' is different.

"Divine works of power reflect the mind and heart of God. They are never pointless spectacles to make people gape. They are life-changing, not mere magic" (Working of Miracles, Charisma Magazine, November 1992, p. 50).

"Miracle" is an over used word in our society. We have miracle drugs, fabrics, detergents, etc. These have all contributed to weakening the understanding of the majesty and power that God shows in genuine miracles.

Real miracle working power operates mainly in the area of meeting a necessity. Most recorded miracles were of supply such as: turning water into wine, multiplying the food, calming the tempest and walking on water.

"Some scholars hold that spectacular, instantaneous healings come under the working of miracles, and gradual healings come under the gifts of healing. It seems to me, however, that the working of miracles operates in the nonhuman creation (inanimate objects, etc.). I feel that if the human body is involved in the working of miracles, it is in some way other than healing. As I see it, all healings come under the gifts of healing. Raising the dead would come under the working of miracles, because in such cases the human body is an inanimate object before being restored to life" (What You Should Know About the Holy Spirit, 1975, p. 123).

When the need is there, the gift is there. It is given as the Holy Spirit sees the need and not before. Working of miracles is part of the package deal given at Pentecost. Every miracle has the fingerprints of God on it. Miracles are unaccountable reverses of the natural order of things that we're accustomed to seeing; they are contrary to the normal.

A miracle is an almighty performance of the Holy Spirit separate from the natural order. A miracle does not have a human explication other than the all-mighty power of our Lord. When in an abrupt and all-powerful act of God steps outside the enclosure by which His beings or nature are surrounded we call it a miracle. This is what God also calls a miracle in His Word.

Stevan F. Williamson brings out an interesting thought in his book, *Who's Afraid of the Holy Ghost?"* "The gift of working of miracles uses an *ordinary* person to create an *extraordinary* event." (*Who's Afraid of the Holy Ghost?* , 1984, p. 165)

God uses humanity to reach humanity. He just needs to find people that are ready to make a courageous step of faith into the miracle arena to perform miracles through their spoken words.

Kinds of Miracles

Miracles as recorded in scripture can apply to nature (Joshua 10:12-14), animals (Numbers 22:28), human beings (Genesis 19:26), nations (Exodus 10:1,2), natural laws (2 Kings 6:5-7), future events (2 Kings 6:8-13), and death (John 11: 41-44).

Some writers like to say that casting out demons is a miracle or healing, when in fact it is deliverance. Deliverance is not listed as a gift of the Holy Spirit. It is the result of the spiritual authority that Christ gave the believer. Deliverance from demons sometimes requires the gifts of healings to accompany it to restore the body or mind back to a normal state. Deliverance from demons also works together with the commanding word of faith. According to Mark 16:17, casting out devils, or demons, should be ordinary believer's work. There is no scriptural reference to having a special ministry or gifting to accomplish deliverance. Pure and simply put, all believers have the right and authority to command demons to leave a person or situation (Matt. 12:29; Matt. 16:19; Luke 10:19).

If miracles defy reason and transcend natural laws, then casting out demons does not qualify as a miracle. *"That at the name of Jesus every knee should bow, of things in heaven, and things in earth, and things under the earth; And that every tongue should confess that Jesus Christ is Lord, to the glory of God the Father"* (Phil 2:10-11).

We have been commanded in John 14-17, to pray to God in the name of Jesus and our prayers would be answered. According to the previous verse, when we command demons to depart in the name of Jesus, we are carrying out instructions to the believers and the results are that the knees bow and tongues confess to the Lordship of Jesus Christ even in the spirit world.

Miracles of Deliverance from Danger

Miracles have been used to deliver and preserve God's people from earliest times. In the Gospels, Jesus was moved with compassion before he performed a miracle (Matthew 18:27; Mark 1:41, etc.).

After Moses led Israel from Egypt to the Red Sea, Pharaoh's army tried to overtake them. The Israelites were surrounded on all sides and pushed up against the Red Sea with no hope of escape in the natural. God provided a supernatural escape through the working of miracles. *"And the LORD said unto Moses, Wherefore criest thou unto me? speak unto the children of Israel, that they go forward: But lift thou up thy rod, and stretch out thine hand over the sea, and divide it: and the children of Israel shall go on dry ground through the midst of the sea"* (Exodus 14:16).

The Red Sea divided and the Israelites crossed over on dry land with the Egyptians in hot pursuit. When the Israelites were all on safe ground, the waters closed in over the top of the Egyptian army. They didn't have any covenant standing with God for their preservation.

110

Paul and Silas found themselves free from prison through a miraculous earthquake. It resulted in the jailer and his whole family being converted to Christ.

"And at midnight Paul and Silas prayed, and sang praises unto God: and the prisoners heard them. And suddenly there was a great earthquake, so that the foundations of the prison were shaken: and immediately all the doors were opened, and every one's bands were loosed. And the keeper of the prison awaking out of his sleep, and seeing the prison doors open, he drew out his sword, and would have killed himself, supposing that the prisoners had been fled. But Paul cried with a loud voice, saying, Do thyself no harm: for we are all here. Then he called for a light, and sprang in, and came trembling, and fell down before Paul and Silas," (Acts 16:25-29).

Miracles of Provision

In the Old Testament God provided miracles many times to sustain individuals and the Israelites. God provided water in the desert, manna, quail and even shoe leather that did not wear out for forty years.

When Jesus walked the earth He used the working of miracles at least twice to feed the multitudes who were both physically and spiritually hungry that had gone into a desert place to hear Him teach.

"When Jesus then lifted up his eyes, and saw a great company come unto him, he saith unto Philip, Whence shall we buy bread, that these may eat? One of his disciples, Andrew, Simon Peter's brother, saith unto him, There is a lad here, which hath five barley loaves, and two small fishes: but what are they among so many? And Jesus said, Make the men sit down. Now there was much grass in the place. So the men sat down, in number about five thousand. And Jesus took the loaves; and when he had given thanks, he distributed to the disciples, and the disciples to them that were set down; and likewise of the fishes as much as they would. When they were filled, he said unto his disciples, Gather up the fragments that remain, that nothing be lost." (John 6:5,8-12)

Miracles Confirm the Word of God

All ten plagues of Egypt were miracles that defied the natural laws of nature to carry out divine judgments and discipline. They were also given for the deliverance and preservation of Israel.

Calling fire down from heaven confirmed to the prophets of Baal and the Israelites who the real God of power was. It helped preserve worship of the one true and living God in a land that had become polluted with idolatry and witchcraft. It also helped confirm God's continuing love and covenant relationship with His people.

After the commission to the believers in Mark 16, as they went throughout the world teaching and preaching, God confirmed their words with miracles and signs.

"And he said unto them, Go ye into all the world, and preach the gospel to every creature. He that believeth and is baptized shall be saved; but he that believeth not shall be damned. And these signs shall follow them that believe; In my name shall they cast out devils; they shall speak with new tongues; They shall take up serpents; and if they drink any deadly thing, it shall not hurt them; they shall lay hands on the sick, and they shall recover. And they went forth, and preached every where, the Lord working with them, and confirming the word with signs following. Amen. (Mark 16:15-18, 20)

Another example of God confirming His Word and power took place when Paul confronted Elymas the sorcerer. The anointing of the Holy Spirit came on Paul and he declared Elymas would be blind for a season to show the superior power that came from God as opposed to Elymas' power source. Elymas' was not blind because of sickness or disease, it was to demonstrate the power of God by the working of miracles at the hand of Paul.

"And when they had gone through the isle unto Paphos, they found a certain sorcerer, a false prophet, a Jew, whose name was Barjesus: Which was with the deputy of the country, Sergius Paulus, a prudent man; who called for Barnabas and Saul, and desired to hear the word of God. But Elymas the sorcerer (for so is his name by interpretation) withstood them, seeking to turn away the deputy from the faith. Then Saul, (who also is called Paul,) filled with the Holy Ghost, set his eyes on him, And said, O full of all subtlety and all mischief, thou child of the devil, thou enemy of all righteousness, wilt thou not cease to pervert the right ways of the Lord? And now, behold, the hand of the Lord is upon thee, and thou shalt be blind, not

seeing the sun for a season. And immediately there fell on him a mist and a darkness; and he went about seeking some to lead him by the hand." (Acts 13:6-11)

The blindness that came on Elymas kept him from hindering the witness of the gospel message by Paul to Sergius Paulus. When Sergius Paulus saw the hand of God, he believed and was converted.

Miracles of Raising the Dead and Restoring the Body

When the gift of working of miracles is used to raise the dead or restore the body, all three power gifts often work together (the gift of faith, the gifts of healings, and the working of miracles). It requires supernatural faith to command a dead body to come back to life. The gift of faith receives a miracle. The working of miracles is needed to restore the decomposing body to a normal state, it works a miracle. The gifts of healing are subsequently required to heal the body of whatever it died of in the first place.

W.V. Grant, a healing evangelist, wrote, "Miracles give power over creation, death, demons and nature. Miracles are performed to deliver people in danger, to perform judgments, to calm storms, to cast out devils, to bind up broken hearts, deliver the captives, and to deliver people from natural stubbornness and rebellion so they may receive the Holy Ghost. Miracles cause people to be saved. Denying miracles does not!" (*The 9 Spiritual Gifts and How To Receive Them*, W.V. Grant, Faith Clinic, Dallas, TX,).

What Do Miracles Produce?

Miracles are signs of God's kingdom and power. They show His mercy, love and wisdom in the affairs of mankind. Miracles always are in character for God. His attributes show that He is a God of might and power. They are designed to bring glory to God.

"Jesus saith unto her, Said I not unto thee, that, if thou wouldest believe, thou shouldest see the glory of God? Then they took away the stone from the place where the dead was laid. And Jesus lifted up his eyes, and said, Father, I thank thee that thou hast heard me. And I knew that thou hearest me always: but because of the people which

113

stand by I said it, that they may believe that thou hast sent me." (John 11:40-42)

Jesus used miracles to draw the attention of people so He could teach them and convince them that He was the Son of God, their Messiah. *"This beginning of miracles did Jesus in Cana of Galilee, and manifested forth his glory; and his disciples believed on him"* (John 2:11).

The miracles were a sign that God was alive among men in the Old Testament (Judges 6:11-24; Exodus 4:2-9; Ex. 16:4; Ex. 17:4-7).

In the New Testament He used miracles to prove that He was a God who had compassion on mankind so much that He sent His only begotten Son to them (Matthew 11:2-5; John 5:36; John 10:41). "Thus Jesus acknowledged that a message confirmed by miracles has greater proof of its authenticity than one without such confirmation" (*Miracles*, Charisma Magazine, Sept. 1992, p. 34).

After the ascension of Christ, the Holy Spirit descended and demonstrated the approval of God on the messengers of the gospel and their message (2 Cor. 12:12; Rom. 15:18,19; John 12:37-41).

His continued miracles today are signs and confirmation that He is still alive among men through the power of the Holy Spirit in them that believe and expect miracles to happen. God will authenticate the divine nature of the gospel until the end of this age when He returns in power and glory.

The Effects Of Miracles On People?

Miracles were a very effective method of convincing some of the Jewish rulers of the ministry of Jesus. *"The same came to Jesus by night, and said unto him, Rabbi, we know that thou art a teacher come from God: for no man can do these miracles that thou doest, except God be with him"* (John 3:2).

Miracles brought forced acknowledgment, amazement, faith and God was glorified as a result (John 11:47; Acts 4:16; Mark 6:49-51; John 2:23; John 11:42; Matthew 9:1-8).

Sign-miracles have a dramatic effect in convincing people of the power of God. Being blinded by God's glory on the Damascas Road during his conversion, had a lasting effect Paul. It became a definite part of the detail when telling of his conversion story to others when he wanted to convince them about God's power.

"*And as he journeyed, he came near Damascus: and suddenly there shined round about him a light from heaven:* (Acts 9:3).

"*And Saul arose from the earth; and when his eyes were opened, he saw no man: but they led him by the hand, and brought him into Damascus. And he was three days without sight, and neither did eat nor drink* (Acts 9:8,9).

"So then, to what kind of people is God's gift of miracles readily available? Those who:

are faithful in what God's called them to do;

are zealous for the gospel;

are serving in situations where miracles are needed to do His work;

are willing to obey the command of Christ;

have compassion for the suffering (*Working of Miracles*, Charisma Magazine, Nov. 1992, p. 51.).

Miracles for Evangelism

"John's Gospel makes it clear that Jesus's miracles were done and recorded to lead people to faith: *Jesus did many other signs in the presence of His disciples, which are not written in this book: but these are written that you may believe that Jesus is the Christ, the Son of God* (John 20:30,31).

"The power of miracles to further the preaching of the gospel is an important theme in the book of Acts:

"At Pentecost, the miraculous descent of the Holy spirit and the resultant tongues-speaking drew the large crowds so that Peter might proclaim the gospel to them (Acts 2).

"When the people saw the lame man healed by Peter walking and praising God, they ran to Solomon's porch where Peter was able to preach to them 3:1-26.

"The apostolic miracles have a similar effect in Acts 5:12-16. That the high priest accused the apostles of filling Jerusalem with their doctrine (5:28) is evidence of the power of the miraculous to open doors for evangelism.

"The city of Samaria listened to Philip because of the miracles

115

they saw him perform (8:6-8).

"When the paralytic Aeneas was healed, Luke notes that: all who dwelt at Lydda and Sharon saw him and turned to the Lord (9:35).

"The raising of Dorcus 'became known throughout all Joppa, and many believed on the Lord.'" (9:42)

"Many Ephesians believed because of the miraculous ministry of the apostle Paul (9:11-20)" (*Miracles*, Charisma Magazine, Sept. 1992, p.35).

"The close connection between miracles and the kingdom finds precise theological formulation in Paul's statement that 'the kingdom of God is not in word but in power:' (I Cor. 4:20). Miraculous power, then, is more than temporary evidence of God's kingdom...it's actually a characteristic of His kingdom" (Ibid, p. 36).

False Miracles

Deceivers will do signs and wonders to try and deceive the very elect in the last days. *"For there shall arise false Christs, and false prophets, and shall show great signs and wonders; insomuch that, if it were possible, they shall deceive the very elect"* (Mat 24:24). This is a good reason why believers do not follow signs, but signs follow believers. Real signs and miracles of God will edify the believer and give glory to God. They will never draw attention to personalities and weird doctrines that contradict the written word of God.

In the final days, before the return of Christ, the anti-christ will use false signs and wonders to draw people to him. He will try to neutralize the faith of Christians by using conjured miracles even as the magicians of Egypt did in the days of Moses (2 Thes. 2:3-9; Rev. 13:13). Jesus predicted these false prophets and anti-christs that would try to take over throughout the ages in Matthew 24:24: "For there shall arise false Christs, and false prophets, and shall show great signs and wonders; insomuch that, if *it were* possible, they shall deceive the very elect."

Miracles of The Bible

The scriptures are full of examples of miracles from the earliest times of the Old Testament to the last narratives of the New Testament. There are actually more accounts of miracles in the Old Testament than in the New Testament. This is possibly because God had already established the fact that He is a miracle working God and there were other things that appeared to be of more importance to the authors of the New Testament. John said that he only recorded a fraction of the many things he saw Jesus do.

"And there are also many other things which Jesus did, the which, if they should be written every one, I suppose that even the world itself could not contain the books that should be written. Amen." (John 21:25)

This does not in any way diminish the working of miracles, they are for the Church today and are still happening all over the world wherever believers are.

The early Church prayed for miracles to happen in their midst.

"And now, Lord, behold their threatenings: and grant unto thy servants, that with all boldness they may speak thy word, By stretching forth thine hand to heal; and that signs and wonders may be done by the name of thy holy child Jesus." (Acts 4:29-30)

As a result, even their deacons were full of the Holy Spirit and worked miracles. *"And Stephen, full of faith and power, did great wonders and miracles among the people"* (Acts 6:8).

Listed below are just some of the many miracles of the Bible:

- Creation - Genesis 1:1-27
- Enoch's translation - Gen. 5:24
- The flood - Gen. 7:17-24
- Confusion of tongues at Babel - Gen. 11: 3-9
- Lot's wife turned to pillar of salt - Gen. 19:26
- Ass speaking - Num. 22:21-25
- Ten plagues of Egypt - Ex.7:20-12:30
- Sun and moon stand still in the valley of Ajalen-Joshua 10:12
- Sun turned back 10 degrees on the sundial.
- Fire falling on Mt. Carmel - 1 Kings 18:38
- Widow's cruse of oil and barrel of meal.- I Kings 17:8-16
- Water turned to wine. - John 2:1-11
- Peter walking on water. - Matthew 14:25-33

- Feeding the multitudes. - Mark 6:35-44
- Raising the dead. - John 11:38-45
- Resurrection of Christ - Luke 24:6; John 10:18
- Dorcus raised from dead - Acts 9:40

Untold thousands of miracles since the Bible has been recorded. They are still happening and will continue until the day of Christ's return.

"Paul urged us in First Corinthians 12:31 to earnestly covet spiritual gifts. When the Church desires to know more about the heart of God, then we will advance higher and learn to become obedient to move in the Spirit where God's power is boundless and His majesty is manifested. We will see greater displays of spiritual gifts than we've ever seen before as we quickly react to God's leading.

CHAPTER 13

THE GIFT OF FAITH

"The Gift of Faith is a gift of the Spirit to the saint that he might work miracles, or rather receive them" (The Gifts of the Spirit, 1946, p. 132).

Faith is one of the three gifts known as the power gifts. It emanates from the Holy Spirit the same as all the other eight gifts of the Spirit. The Holy Spirit's gift of faith can accomplish things that our faith cannot because of our lack of development. The Holy Spirit's faith has no limitations from doubt or ignorance of God's Word and can intervene at the most crucial times to empower the believer to receive an answer to a need or petition. This type of faith is not something that can be developed for everyday living. Our day to day faith comes from God's Word. *So then faith cometh by hearing, and hearing by the Word of God"* (Romans 10: 17).

The fruit of faith grows character. The gift of faith, because it is a gift, cannot be obtained or earned by man's efforts.

Hebrews 11:1, explains faith as the power to possess that which we do not see with our natural eyes. The opening phrase of this verse is, *"Now faith is."* Faith always operates in the present tense relating to things that will be manifest in the future. The object of our faith is totally unseen now, but we are totally convinced, without wavering, that it is a reality and will be manifest in its proper time. The immaterial becomes actual substance through the active power of faith.

"Jesus said unto him, If thou canst believe, all things are possible to him that believeth" (Mark 9:23).

This miraculous faith is just a small portion of God's total faith. Because it is one of the gifts of the Holy Spirit, it works under the anointing of the Holy Spirit.

"Jesus answering, saith unto them, Have faith in God. For verily I say unto you, That whosoever shall say unto this mountain, Be thou removed, and be thou cast into the sea; and shall not doubt in his heart, but shall believe that those things which he saith shall come to pass; he shall have whatsoever he saith. Therefore I say unto you, 'What things soever ye desire, when ye pray, believe that ye receive them, and ye shall have them'." (Mark 11:22-24)

We clearly are taught by Jesus to speak out what is believed so that it can happen. These verses have come under attack by a variety of persons who want to complicate the message of faith. Faith is so simple that often it is bypassed as almost nonessential or on the other end of the pendulum, it is made so difficult to attain that only a privileged few can ever attain the spiritual level required to have real faith.

If we want something that is according to the Will and Word of God we must first ask for it. Then we must believe in our heart that we already have it and continue to speak about it as a reality.

God has promised healing, He wants all mankind to be saved, He wants to meet our need financially and set people free from the bondages of the enemy. The gift of faith gives a person the ability to receive each of these.

"The gift of faith hinges on speaking. The scriptural pattern of the operation of faith through speaking began at creation. *"And God said, Let there be light: and there was light"* (Gen. 1:3).

God's faith is always expressed through the words He speaks. When He speaks, His words come to pass.

"Through faith we understand that the worlds were framed by the word of God, so that things which are seen were not made of things which do appear." (Heb. 11:3)

"For I am the LORD: I will speak, and the word that I shall speak shall come to pass; it shall be no more prolonged: for in your days, O rebellious house, will I say the word, and will perform it, saith the Lord GOD." (Ezek. 12:25)

"*Infusion* is a term that best describes the dynamic at work in the gift of faith. Besides revealing His immediate will through a vision or inner voice, God also gives an infusion of calm, power and confidence—an internal knowledge that the act of God is coming to pass as the spoken words proclaim it" (Ibid. p. 38).

Hebrews 11 lists some of the Old Testament examples of miracles brought about by faith:

"Who through faith subdued kingdoms, wrought righteousness, obtained promises, stopped the mouths of lions, Quenched the violence of fire, escaped the edge of the sword, out of weakness were made strong, waxed valiant in fight, turned to flight the armies of the aliens. Women received their dead raised to life again: and others were tortured, not accepting deliverance; that they might obtain a better resurrection:" (Heb. 11:33-35)

The basic rules of faith are simple. Jesus taught about faith and often rebuked the disciples for not having even the simple faith of a little child. When a child sets his mind on something, nothing else in the world matters. His mind is made up and he is totally convinced he will receive what he wants. He will continue to speak about his desire until it is given to him. That is the way we must be about the things we ask for by faith in God's Word.

"The gift of faith brings forth a spring of belief from within and propels us to operate in the supernatural realm. It is a present-tense faith, sensing that God will make a special event happen, knowing that nothing is impossible" (The Gift of Faith, Charisma Magazine, Nov. 1992, p. 37).

"And Jesus said unto them, Because of your unbelief: for verily I say unto you, If ye have faith as a grain of mustard seed, ye shall say unto this mountain, Remove hence to yonder place; and it shall remove; and nothing shall be impossible unto you." (Mat. 17:20)

Four Kinds of Faith

Natural Faith:

We have a certain amount of natural faith in the things that are in our world because of our past experience with them. We have faith that our car is going to start with a certain key when we turn it. We have faith that the light is going to go on when we flick the switch. We have faith that daylight is going to follow the darkness or spring is going to follow the winter season. Why? Because we've had time to experience these and we know that if all is going as it should, these things will follow as results. We hardly even think of them. In our lives these things do not require much deliberation, they just happen.

Saving Faith:

This type of faith is given to each person who comes to Jesus and chooses him as their Savior. *"But as many as received him, to them gave he power to become the sons of God, even to them that believe on his name": (John 1:12).*

Romans 12:3, teaches about the measure of faith that each is given at the time of salvation. This shows that God is an equal opportunity God. He gives each the same measure to start their faith journey. The most significant part to this is that the growth possibilities are limitless. *"For by grace are ye saved through faith; and that not of yourselves: it is the gift of God: Not of works, lest any man should boast" (Ephesians 2:8,9).*

Paul instructs this faith is a gift of God. Faith cannot be earned or gotten by merit. Faith must be acted on to attain the gift of salvation that is also a free gift from God. After the initial salvation experience, this faith needs to be activated on a daily basis for the person to come before the throne of God boldly and receive continuous cleansing from any unrighteousness that tries to creep back and separate the person from God again. *"But if we walk in the light, as he is in the light, we have fellowship one with another, and the blood of Jesus Christ his Son cleanseth us from all sin"* (1 John 1:7).

"...Believe on the Lord Jesus Christ, and thou shalt be saved, and thy house" (Acts 16:31). This promise is to the believer who, if he will stand firmly in faith, both he and his entire household will be saved. The same promise given to the jailer in this passage is applicable to each today who wants to take it and stand without wavering for their family. God is no respecter of persons, therefore what He offers to one person, He gladly offers to all.

Faith As A Fruit of the Spirit:

The fruit of the Spirit mentioned in Galatians 5:22 is for building up a person's character. This is God's improvement plan for humanity. The gifts will all pass away some day when we see Jesus face to face, but the fruit of the Spirit will last forever in our improved character if we've allowed them to be nourished properly. Some people are more interested in just becoming a character than they are in allowing the Holy Spirit to groom their character.

"I am the vine, ye are the branches: He that abideth in me, and I in him, the same bringeth forth much fruit: for without me ye can do nothing" (John 15:5). This is talking about the fruit of faith or faithfulness that flourishes after it goes through a pruning process. All the excesses are snipped and the branch produces better, healthier fruit as a result.

The Gift of Faith that is a grace gift
(1 Corinthians 12:9):

This gift of faith trusts God for what seems impossible to the natural mind and eye. Often the gift of faith is so integrated into the other gifts it is almost impossible to separate them. The gift of faith is actually the catalyst that many times enables other gifts to work.

Significantly this is the only gift that is also listed among the fruit, although we have already seen that there is a difference between this faith and the fruit of faith. The fruit of faith is for character and this faith is for power. There is a progression of where these areas of faith come into a person's life First, there is faith for salvation, after salvation comes faith for the refining of the character, after the baptism in the Holy Spirit, as one enters the walk of the gifts of the Spirit, comes faith as an empowering gift.

The gift of faith is distinct from the gift of working of miracles, but both produce miracles. The gift of working of miracles is more active, whereas the gift of faith is often described as passive. Although there is also a certain amount of activity that accompanies faith. Faith is distinct from the gift of healing, but both can produce healing. The gift of faith's power receives or enjoys things by the Spirit.

Daniel 6:17-28 is a good example of the gift of faith given to Daniel in his time of crisis. The fact that he remained intact in the pit with the fierce beasts all night was a miracle brought about by the gift of faith.

"And a stone was brought, and laid upon the mouth of the den; and the king sealed it with his own signet, and with the signet of his lords; that the purpose might not be changed concerning Daniel. Then the king went to his palace, and passed the night fasting: neither were instruments of music brought before him: and his sleep went from him. Then the king arose very early in the morning, and went in haste unto the den of lions. And when he came to the den, he cried with a lamentable voice unto Daniel: and the king spake and said to Daniel, O Daniel, servant of the living God, is thy God, whom thou servest continually, able to deliver thee from the lions? Then said Daniel unto the king, O king, live for ever. My God hath sent his angel, and hath shut the lions' mouths, that they have not hurt me: forasmuch as before him innocency was found in me; and also before thee, O king, have I done no hurt. Then was the king exceeding glad for him, and commanded that they should take Daniel up out of the den. So Daniel was taken up out of the den, and no manner of hurt was found upon him, because he believed in his God. And the king commanded, and they brought those men which had accused Daniel, and they cast them into the den of lions, them, their children, and their wives; and the lions had the mastery of them, and brake all their bones in pieces or ever they came at the bottom of the den. Then king Darius wrote unto all people, nations, and languages, that dwell in all the earth; Peace be multiplied unto you. I make a decree, That in every dominion of my kingdom men tremble and fear before the God of Daniel: for he is the living God, and steadfast for ever, and his kingdom that which shall not be destroyed, and his dominion shall be even unto the end. He delivereth and rescueth, and he worketh signs and wonders in heaven and in earth, who hath delivered Daniel from the power of the lions. So this Daniel prospered in the reign of Darius, and in the reign of Cyrus the Persian." (Dan 6:17-28)

Mark 4:35-41, tells the story of the disciples during a storm on the sea. If they had remained calm and refused fear to rob and intimidate them, they would have weathered it by a miracle of faith in the words that Jesus had spoken to them before they started. He said they were going to cross over to the other side. At His word they could have crossed over through the storm as though it did not exist.

They had taken Him at His word earlier and cast their nets over the sides and taken in a big catch of fish. However, because Jesus could not get them to trust Him in the storm, He needed to remove it by a word of faith as He spoke to the storm and rebuked it, demanding it cease to exist.

"And the same day, when the even was come, he saith unto them, Let us pass over unto the other side. And when they had sent away the multitude, they took him even as he was in the ship. And there were also with him other little ships. And there arose a great storm of wind, and the waves beat into the ship, so that it was now full. And he was in the hinder part of the ship, asleep on a pillow: and they awake him, and say unto him, Master, carest thou not that we perish? And he arose, and rebuked the wind, and said unto the sea, Peace, be still. And the wind ceased, and there was a great calm. And he said unto them, Why are ye so fearful? how is it that ye have no faith? And they feared exceedingly, and said one to another, What manner of man is this, that even the wind and the sea obey him?" (Mark 4:35-41)

This kind of faith openly displays the power of God as He honors the words of faith spoken by people and brings into existence something that was not manifested before speaking them. Sometimes these are manifested immediately while others can take a period of time before they are seen. Jesus spoke to the fig tree and commanded that it dry up. It began immediately to die at the roots but took several days to be noticed outwardly by the disciples.

"And when he saw a fig tree in the way, he came to it, and found nothing thereon, but leaves only, and said unto it, Let no fruit grow on thee henceforward for ever. And presently the fig tree withered away" (Mat 21:19).

Faith is a necessity in the operation of all the other gifts of the Spirit. The gift of faith is a specific supernatural gifting that only comes from the hand of God. It is equally as important as the other eight gifts of the Spirit. Although it is difficult to explain because it cannot be seen, it is definitely witnessed in the spirit of the individual when it is present and active. There is optimism or reassurance of knowing that the desired result is accomplished even without seeing any outward signs. Jesus taught that we will do great things through faith.

THE GIFTS OF THE HOLY SPIRIT ARE FOR YOU!

"Believe me that I am in the Father and the Father in me: or else believe me for the very works; sake. Verily, verily, I say unto you, He that believeth on me, the works that I do shall he do also; and greater works than these shall he do; because I go unto my Father. And whatsoever ye shall ask in my name, that will I do, that the Father may be glorified in the Son. If ye shall ask any thing in my name, I will do it. If ye love me, keep my commandments. And I will pray the Father, and he shall give you another Comforter, that he may abide with you for ever;" (John 14:11-16)

The key to operating in the gift of faith is a living relationship with the Holy Spirit brought about through prayer, walking in the anointing and consistently reading the Word of God. We are to hold fast to our profession of faith without wavering, and the Lord who is faithful will do it.

"Let us hold fast the profession of our faith without wavering; (for he is faithful that promised;) And let us consider one another to provoke unto love Lord said, If ye had faith as a grain of mustard seed, ye night say unto this sycamine tree, Be thou plucked up by the root, and be thou planted in the sea; and it should obey you." (Luke 17:6)

Miracle Faith

How much faith does one need for a miracle? Only the size of a mustard seed is sufficient to do great things. Faith grows like a mustard seed if it is planted in good soil. When beginning our spiritual journey, we discover we have very limited faith. The more we hear the Word of God and learn to hear the Lord's voice, the more we grow in areas of faith. Everything that we receive from God's Word is contingent on what is done with it. Believing and speaking according to God's Word will decide whether a person has more or less of anything. Faith must be cultivated. Nobody can give faith to someone else by praying for them. Faith comes by hearing the Word of God and then acting on it.

No one can stockpile faith in a tin boxes and put them on the shelf for later. It is an active ingredient. It is much like yeast in bread. Yeast will activate like it is supposed to if it is fresh and in full of power. It will turn into a hard lump and eventually die if it is not used while the ingredients are still alive.

When the gift of faith is activated in our spirit, we have a certainty that we know, that we know, that we know, what we have spoken will certainly come to pass. During our years as missionaries in Nicaragua, Central America I had been praying for healing from what had started as a small rash under my wedding ring and escalated into a full-blown case of "galloping eczema" that was spreading all over my body. The doctors put me on heavy maintenance drugs and said I would have to take them for life. I kept praying that God would heal me night after night.

One night we were in a little border town close to Honduras where Jerry, my husband, was preaching. Nothing was different from any other night. He spoke the same basic message of faith and healing, but that night there was an assurance of faith in my spirit and I knew without a doubt that I was completely healed of that horrible disease that had plagued me for several years.

I did not look any different. My hands were still raw and looked terrible, but I knew with an unshakable certainty that I would never need the medicine again. I declared it so on the way home that night. I was so excited because I knew the work had been done. Within the week my skin healed completely of all the ravages of eczema and there has never been a recurrence. It was a healing that started with a gift of faith that was the catalyst for the total manifestation to come into being. When the gift of faith is in operation, a person has such an assurance of God's Will and purposes that God honors their words as they speak unseen things into existence.

Biblical Examples of the Gift of Faith

Blessings:

The Bible gives us other examples to help us better understand this mighty gift of power. Faith filled words were spoken many times and God brought them to pass just as they were uttered. Blessings were spoken over children and fulfilled by God. *"By faith, Isaac blessed Jacob and Esau concerning things to come" (Hebrews 11: 20; Genesis 27).*

Isaac, who was along in years, had poor eyesight and became

the object of parental favoritism. His wife and youngest son betrayed him into giving a blessing. He thought it was to Esau, the elder of the two, but it was spoken over Jacob and became the divine plan of God for Jacob's life instead.

Jacob, before his death, gave a blessing over his grandsons, Efraim and Manassah. At the last second he crossed his arms and gave the greater blessing to the youngest, contrary to traditions of that day. He also spoke blessings and prophecy over his other sons and their tribes, which have come to pass over the years of history.

Personal Protection In Perilous Times:

For protection in perilous times we see the three Hebrew children mentioned in Daniel's day. They spoke a miracle into existence by faith that put the fourth man in the fiery furnace with them and they were delivered from the fire and their bondages.

Daniel in the lion's den has already been mentioned. That was a miracle of preservation from certain death in the jaws of fierce beasts.

Faith For Receiving The Astounding Promises Of God:

Abraham, was 100 years old when his son of promise was born to him. The Bible says that, *"He staggered not at the promises of God through unbelief; but was strong in faith, giving glory to God" (Romans 4:20; Gen. 21:5).* It took him twenty-five years of resting in faith for that word to happen. God is not on a twenty-four hour time clock. However we note that the timing of the fulfillment came into swift movement when Abraham and Sarah's names were changed. Each time Abraham was called he was acknowledging he was the "father of many nations."

One night after being in an open-air crusade meeting my husband, Jerry, had his trumpet stolen in Nicaragua many years ago. The gift of faith came up in him immediately and he spoke out of his mouth that the trumpet would be returned. People suggested he should send to the U.S. for another horn, because the one he had was gone forever. Things were not normally recovered once they disappeared in Latin America. His reply was, "I do not need another horn, I have got trumpet. It's not in my hands at this minute, but I already have a trumpet."

In a city of nearly a million inhabitants, he was speaking the impossible to the ears of his listeners, but he believed that the God of the impossible would make it possible. He had an unshakable faith in God's provision. A few weeks later he went to the very house where his trumpet was and recuperated it from a man that had bought it from the thief. He was able to prove his ownership by some photos he had and recoup his trumpet just as the Holy Spirit has assured him he would.

Supernatural Victory In The Fight:
Faith gives us supernatural victory in the fight. *"And it came to pass, when Moses held up his hand, that Israel prevailed: and when he let down his hand, Amalek prevailed"* (Exodus 17:11). Aaron and Hur held up the hands of Moses until the victory was won. Their faith was in the fact that as long as Moses' arms were upraised, they would win, and they did.

There would be more victories today, if instead of cynically making fun of people, the church would provide more Aaron and Hurs to hold up the modern day Moses' hands in the middle of conflict. More people are needed to sustain each other in the battle.

Supernatural Faith In Domestic Problems:
A widow was threatened by creditors. Her sons were going to have to go to jail to pay her debts. She went to Elisha, the prophet. with her problem. It's possible her husband had been one of his prophet-students. Because all she had was a pot of oil, the prophet used what she had. He spoke a word of faith over the situation and she poured out and sold enough oil to pay all her bills off. As long as she maintained faith in what was spoken, and gathered enough pots, the oil poured and poured. When she stopped, the miracle stopped.

This word of faith is seen supplying supernatural sustenance when a widow and her son were commanded to make the first cake for the prophet. She found that as long as she made one for him first, she never ran out of supply. She acted by faith on his word of faith and they all made it through the famine.

"And the word of the LORD came unto him, saying, Arise, get thee to Zarephath, which belongeth to Zidon, and dwell there: behold, I have commanded a widow woman there to sustain thee. So he arose and went to Zarephath. And when he came to the gate of the city, behold, the widow woman was there gathering of sticks: and he called to her, and said, Fetch me, I pray thee, a little water in a vessel, that I may drink. And as she was going to fetch it, he called to her, and said, Bring me, I pray thee, a morsel of bread in thine hand. And she said, As the LORD thy God liveth, I have not a cake, but an handful of meal in a barrel, and a little oil in a cruse: and, behold, I am gathering two sticks, that I may go in and dress it for me and my son, that we may eat it, and die. And Elijah said unto her, Fear not; go and do as thou hast said: but make me thereof a little cake first, and bring it unto me, and after make for thee and for thy son. For thus saith the LORD God of Israel, The barrel of meal shall not waste, neither shall the cruse of oil fail, until the day that the LORD sendeth rain upon the earth. And she went and did according to the saying of Elijah: and she, and he, and her house, did eat many days. And the barrel of meal wasted not, neither did the cruse of oil fail, according to the word of the LORD, which he spake by Elijah/" (1 Ki 17:8-16)

The Gift Of Faith To Deal With Evil Spirits:
The gift of faith is used also to cast out evil spirits. Jesus spoke and cast the evil spirits out with his word. In these cases we can see the gift of discerning of spirits and the gift of the word of knowledge working with the gift of faith. Often several gifts will intertwine and work together.

Persons were delivered from demons or healed by taking prayer soaked fabrics and putting them on the sick or troubled person. Cancers have been known to fall off persons in the hospitals when a cloth was given to them that had been anointed and prayed over. A gift of faith goes into operation when these objects are declared to be the contact point of faith for the person receiving them. God still honors this method today, just as He did in the book of Acts. *"So that from his body were brought unto the sick handkerchiefs or aprons, and the diseases departed from them, and the evil spirits went out of them"* *(Acts 19:12).*

Many times people have prayed over the pillowcases of their

loved ones and God has done miracles, honoring their declaration of faith. This gift may seem less spectacular than some other gifts of the Spirit. Faith is sometimes manifested secretly or silently over long periods, but that does not make it any less supernatural. Active faith always moves God. The results always bring honor and glory to God.

The Gift Of Faith To Raise The Dead:

It takes a gift of faith to raise the dead. Every funeral Jesus ever attended or came upon, He raised the dead. Lazarus, Jairus' daughter and the widow of Nain's son were all raised by a word of faith and a creative miracle. Dorcus was raised by the gift of faith, healing, and a miracle. Paul raised a young man up whom fatally fell from a window during a long church service. *"For it is God which worketh in you both to will and to do of his good pleasure"* (Phil. 2:13). *"But without faith, it is impossible to please him, for he that cometh to God must believe that he is, and that he is a rewarder of them that diligently seek him"* (Hebrews 11:6).

The potential of the gift of faith is present in every believer from the time of salvation, but like all the other gifts, they are in greater manifestation after the baptism of the Holy Spirit occurs.

The Gift Of Faith Brings Correction:

The gift of faith administered spiritual correction to some youths who were killed by a wild beast for mocking God's prophet.

"And he went up from thence unto Bethel: and as he was going up by the way, there came forth little children out of the city, and mocked him, and said unto him, Go up, thou bald head; go up, thou bald head. And he turned back, and looked on them, and cursed them in the name of the LORD. And there came forth two she bears out of the wood, and tare forty and two children of them." (2 Ki 2:23-24)

Paul had Elymus, the sorcerer, struck blind once by speaking a word of faith. Peter pronounced judgment on Ananias and Saphira by a word of faith and they dropped dead on the spot.

"The gift of faith rests on knowing the will of God. This may come by special revelation, such as dreams, visions, etc; it may come by the inner voice of the Spirit; or by the written Word of God, quickened for specific direction. It operates on the same principle as all faith as revealed in Romans 10:17. The sure knowledge of His will produces absolute faith. *'This is the confidence we have in Him, that if we ask anything according to His will, He heareth us.'* (1 John 5:14)" (The Holy Spirit Today, 1976, p. 83).

"So then faith cometh by hearing, and hearing by the word of God" (Rom 10:17).

Bibliography

Barclift, Mark A. "Understanding the Gift: Word of Knowledge." Paraclete. Summer 1985. pp. 26-28.

Bonnke, Reinhard. "Working of Miracles." Charisma Magazine. November 1992. pp. 49-51.

Bullinger, Ethelbert W. A Critical Lexicon and Concordance to the English and Greek New Testament. Grand Rapids, MI. Zondervan Publishing House.1979.

Carlson, G. Raymond. "The Role of the Prophet Today." Pentecostal Evangel. Springfield, MO. August 5, 1990.

"Christian's Place In The Church, The". Volume 3, Adult Teacher. Springfield, MO. Radiant Life. 1987. pp.352-354.

Conner, Kevin, J. Interpreting the Symbols and Types. Portland, OR. Bible Temple Publications. 1980.

Copeland, Gloria. "The Power of Praying In Tongues." Voice of Victory Magazine. September 1992.

Gaglardi, Maureen. The Path of the Just. Volume I. Vancouver, B.C. Canada. New West Press Co. 1963. p. 131.

De Arteaga, William. "Quenching The Holy Spirit." Charisma Magazine. September 1992. pp. 46-54.

Deere, Jack. "Cultivating The Spirit's Gifts." Charisma Magazine. September 1993. pp. 60-70.

Deere, Jack. "Miracles." Charisma Magazine. September 1992. pp.31-35.

Gee, Donald. Concerning Spiritual Gifts. Springfield, MO. Radient Books. 1949.

Gill, A.L. and Gill, Joyce. Supernatural Living Through the Gifts of the Holy Spirit. Fawnskin, CA. Powerhouse Publishing.1988. p. 110.

Hagin, Kenneth E. "The Working of Miracles." The Word of Faith Magazine. April 1992. pp. 4-10.

Hagin, Kenneth E. "The Value of Tongues, Part I and II." The Word of Faith Magazine. February/March 1995.

Hagin Jr., Kenneth. "Preparing Ourselves For the Move of God's Sprit." The Word of Faith Magazine. January 1992. pp. 15-17.

Hayford, Jack. "Though I Speak In Tongues." Charisma Magazine. March 1993. pp. 31-37.

Horton, Harold. The Gifts of the S pirit. Bedfordshire, England. Redemption Tidings Bookroom. 1946.

Holdcroft, L. Thomas. The Holy Spirit. Springfield, MO. Gospel Publishing House. 1962.

Iverson, Dick. The Holy Spirit Today. Portland, OR. The Center Press. 1976.

Joyner, Rick. "The Revolution Is At Hand." The Morning Star. Vol. 2. No. 1. 1992. pp. 51-61.

Jepson, J.W. What You Should Know About The Holy Spirit. Beavercreek, OR. Bible Voice, Inc. 1975. pp.111-130.

King, Jeff. "Guidelines for the Prophetic Word." Ministries Today. July/August 1994. pp. 54-59.

Lance, Fran and Lawless, Agnes. The Gifts of the Spirit. Edmonds, WA. AglowPublications. 1974.

Lim, David. Spiritual Gifts, A Fresh Look. Springfield, MO. Gospel Publishing House. 1991.

MacNutt, Judith. "Discerning of Spirits." Charisma Magazine. November 1992. pp.57-60.

Mahesh, Chasda. "The Gift of Faith." Charisma Magazine. November 1992.

Menzies, William W. Bible Doctrines, A Pentecostal Perspective. Springfield, MO. Logion Press. 1993. p. 126.

New Bible Dictionary, The. Grand Rapids, MI. Wm. B. Eerdmans Publishing Co. 1962.

Nuzum, Mrs. C. The Life of Faith. Springfield, MO. Gospel Publishing House. 1928.

Palma, Anthony D. "Distinguishing of Spirits." Advance. November 1993. pp. 16-17.

Palma, Anthony D. "Baptized by and in the Holy Spirit." Advance. August 1994. pp. 16-17.

Palma, Anthony D. "Glossolalia—do Luke and Paul agree?" Advance. May 1994. pp. 18-19.

Pearlman, Myer. The Heavenly Gift, Studies In The Work of the Holy Spirit. Springfield, MO. Gospel Publishing House. 1935. p.20.

Pearlman, Myer and Boyd, Frank M. Pentecostal Truth. Springfield, MO. Gospel Publishing House. 1968.

Pearson, Mark A. "Gifts of Healings." Charisma Magazine. November 1992. pp. 41-43.

Riggs, Ralph M. The Spirit Himself. Springfield, MO, Gospel Publishing House. 1949.

Ragont, Joe. Basic Bible Doctrine - The Holy Spirit. Chicago, IL. Moody Bible Institute. 1978. pp.1-8.

Rowlands, Rev. Gerald. How to know The Fullness of the Spirit. Lynnwood, WA. Women's Aglow Fellowship. 1982. pp. 20-32.

Simpson, A.B. The Gospel of Healing. Harrisburg, PA. Christian Publications, Inc.1915.

Simpson, A.B. The Holy Spirit, Volumes 1 and 2. Harrisburg, PA. Christian Publications, Inc.

Stamps, Donald C. The Full Life Study Bible. Grand Rapids, MI. Zondervan Publishing House.1985. pp. 1790-1791, 1840-41.

Wagner, C. Peter. Your Spiritual Gifts Can Help Your Church Grow. Ventura, CA. Regal Books. 1982.

Williams, J. Redman. "Gifts of the Spirit." Charisma Magazine. November 1992. p. 27.

Williamson, Stevan F. Who's Afraid of the Holy Ghost? Tulsa, OK. Harrison House, Inc. 1994.

"Understanding the Work of the Spirit." Volume 7 Adult Teacher. Springfield, MO. Gospel Publishing House. 1977. pp. 356-365.

Zodhiates Th.D., Spiros. The Complete Word Study Dictionary, New Testament. Chattanooga, TN. AMG Publishers. 1992.

THE GIFTS OF THE HOLY SPIRIT ARE FOR YOU!

Additional References

Anderson, Paul. "Your Sons & Daughters Shall Prophecy." Charisma Magazine. June 1985.

Arrington, French L. The Acts of the Apostles. Peabody, MH. Hendrickson Publishers, Inc. 1988.

Basham, Don. A Handbook on Holy Spirit Baptism. Springdale, PA. Whitaker House. 1969.

Bennett, Dennis. How to Pray for the Release of the Holy Spirit. South Plainfield, NJ. Bridge Publishing, Inc. 1985.

Benson, Litt.D., Clarence H. The Triune God. Wheaton, IL. Evangelical Teacher Training Association. 1970.

Cain, Paul. "The Anointing VS Respectability." The Morning Star. Pineville, NC. Volume 2, No. 1. 1990. pp. 36-44.

Copeland, Gloria. And Jesus Healed Them All. Fort Worth, TX. Kenneth Copeland   Ministries. 1981.

Copeland, Gloria. Walk in the Spirit. Fort Worth, TX. KCP Publications.1984.

Dake, Finis Jennings. Bible Truths Unmasked. Lawrenceville, GA, Bible Research
          Foundations, Inc. 1950.

Dalton, Robert Chandler. Tongues Like As Of Fire. Springfield, MO. Gospel Publishing House. 1945.

Grodsham, Stanley H. With Signs Following. Springfield, MO. Gospel Publishing House, 1946.

Grant. W.V. The 9 Spiritual Gifts and How To Receive Them. Dallas, TX. Faith Clinic.

Green, Sr. Jay P. The Interlinear Greek-English New Testament Volume 5. Peabody, MA. Hendrickson Publishers. 1980.

Grudem, Ph.D., Dr. Wayne. "Does God Still Give Revelation Gifts?" Charisma Magazine. September 1992.

Groves, H. MIRACLE Healing. Tulsa, OK.

Hagin, Kenneth E. The Key To Scriptural Healing. Tulsa, OK. Kenneth Hagin Evangelistic Association. 1977.

Hagin, Kenneth E. Exceedingly Growing Faith. Tulsa, OK. RHEMA Bible Church. 1983.

Hagin, Kenneth E. A Fresh Anointing. Tulsa, OK. Faith Library Publications. 1990.

Hagin, Kenneth E. "Faith for Receiving the Baptism in the Holy Spirit." The Word of Faith Magazine. August 1989. pp. 12-17.

Hagin, Kenneth E. "Healing God's Will for You." The Word of Faith Magazine. Tulsa, OK. December 1989. pp. 14-17.

Hagin, Kenneth E. "The Doctrine of Laying on of Hands." The Word of Faith Magazine. Tulsa, OK. May 1990. pp. 4-7.

Hagin, Kenneth E. Understanding the Anointing. Tulsa, OK. Faith Library Publications. 1983.

Hammerle, David C. "How Does God Feel About Speaking in Tongues?" Advance. June 1995. pp. 6-7.

Hamon, Bill. "Personal Prophecy." Charisma Magazine. April 1991.

Hayford, Jack. "Tongues & Interpretation." Charisma Magazine. November 1992. pp. 63-66.

Hays, Norvel. The Gifts of Healing. Tulsa, OK. Harrison House. 1980.

Hays, Norvel. The Gift of Working of Miracles. Tulsa, OK. Harrison House. 1980.

Hays, Norvel. Endued with Power. Tulsa, OK. Harrison House.1991.

Hickey, Marilyn. BE HEALED. Denver, CO. Marilyn Hickey Ministries. 1992.

Hickey, Marilyn. "Pointers On Prophecy." Charisma Magazine. January 1986.

Hinn, Benny. "Capturing The Anointing." Celebrate Jesus. Volume 4. 1990.

Horton, Stanley M. "Divine Healing." Pentecostal Evangel. Springfield, MO. September 17, 1995. p. 12.

Hunter, Charles and Hunter, Francis. Handbook for Healing. Kingwood, TX. Hunter Books. 1987.

Hunter, Charles and Hunter, Francis. How To Heal The Sick. Kingwood, TX. Hunter Books. 1981.

Johnson, Bernhard. The Work of An Evangelist. Minneapolis, MN. World Wide Publications. 1984.

THE GIFTS OF THE HOLY SPIRIT ARE FOR YOU!

Lindsay, Gordon. All About The Gifts of the Spirit. Dallas, TX. The World Correspondence Course. 1962.

Nave's Topical Bible. Chicago, IL. Moody Press. 1974.

Osteen, John. How to Flow in the Super Super Natural. Houston, TX. John Osteen Publications. 1978.

Price, Frederick K.C. How Faith Works. Tulsa, OK. Harrison House. 1976.

Ravenhill, Leonard. "God Is Looking For Men." The Morning Star. Vol.2. pp. 45-50.

Renner, Rick. Merchandising the Anointing. Tulsa, OK. Rick Renner Ministries. 1990.

Renner, Rick. Seducing Spirits and Doctrines of Demons. Tulsa, OK. Pillar Books. 1988.

Rowlands, Rev. Gerald. How to be Alive in the Spirit. Lynnwood, WA. Women's Aglow Publications. 1982.

Savelle, Jerry. "Your Precious Heritage of Faith." Victory Magazine. 1993.

Sekowsky, Jo Anne. The Holy Spirit. Lynnwood, WA. Aglow Publications, Inc. 1980.

Thigpen, Paul. "Did The Power of the Spirit Ever Leave The Church?" Charisma Magazine. September 1992. pp. 20-29.

Wagner, C. Peter. "The Gift of Prophecy is for Today." Ministries Today. Jan/Feb 1987.

Wimber, John. "The Gift of Prophecy." Charisma Magazine. November 1992.

Zodhiates, Th.D., Spiros. The Hebrew-Greek Key Study Bible. Grand Rapids, MI. Baker Book House. 1984.

Shiloh Publishing House Materials

BOOKS
Strongman's His Name, What's His Game?......................$13.95
Strongman's His Name II....................................$13.95
Trust God, He Really Does Love You..........................$13.95
Strongman's His Name Laminated Reference Card............$4.00
Spanish Strongman's His Name I Book............................$10.95
French Strongman's His Name I Book............................$10.95
Suddenly, One Was Taken (A Novel)............................$9.00
Faith In Eruption..$1.00
Knee-Deep In The Soup & Other Stupid Stories (Teens).$10.00
Mighty Warriors Jr. Activity/Coloring Book (Children's)..$8.00

VIDEOS
8-Hour Live Strongman Seminar on Video....................$149.95
1-Hour, "Riding In The Chariot To Victory"........................$20.00

CASSETTE TAPES

Single Tape:
Verses of Praise from the Psalms (30 minutes)....................$3.00
Can Satan Understand Tongues or Read Your Mind?..............$5.00
Conquering the Giants of Your Life............................$5.00
False Prophecy Unmasked......................................$5.00
God's Royal Road to Spiritual Success........................$5.00
How to Receive Your Prayer Language..........................$5.00
Rise and Be Healed!..$5.00
Run to Win!..$5.00
Spirit, Soul & Body..$5.00
The Holy Spirit In Esther....................................$5.00
The Mystery of Job...$5.00
What's Wrong with Rock Music?................................$5.00

2-Cassette Series:
Good Things Come From God....................................$10.00
Victory Over Fear..$10.00

THE GIFTS OF THE HOLY SPIRIT ARE FOR YOU!

<u>4-Cassette Series:</u>
6-Hour Live Strongman Seminar..$20.00
Seven Ministry Gifts to Success...$20.00
The Nine Gifts of the Holy Spirit $20.00
The Fruit of the Spirit...$20.00

<u>6-Cassette Series:</u>
Strongman I Read onto Cassette with Outline Booklet........ $30.00

<u>12-Cassette Series:</u>
Delux Gifts Set composed of three 4-Cassette series: 7 Ministry
Gifts to Success, The 9 Gifts of the Holy Spirit aqnd The Fruit of
the Spirit. This is a power-packed album!...............................$45.00

Delux Victory Set composed of: Strongman I "book on tape" 6-
cassette series, The 9 Gifts of the Holy Spirit and Victory Over
Fear series. Includes two booklets......................................$50.00

Payment in U.S. dollars must accompany orders. Please include
postage from chart below. Make all checks payable to Shiloh
Publishing House. Master Card and Visa are accepted with the
number and expiration date.

For a current catalog or to make an order please mail to:
Shiloh Publishing House
P.O. Box 100
Woodburn, OR 97071

To phone an order call between 9 a.m. and 5 p.m. Pacific Time.
(800) 607-6195

Postage Charges on Orders in the U.S.A.	
Up to $4.99......$1.50	$50 to $100.........5.00
$5 to $16.99.....$2.25	$101 to $150.....$7.50
$17 to $29.99...$2.85	Over $150.....$7.50 Plus add
$30 to 49.99....$3.25	$1.00 per each additional $35.
	of merchandise.
These prices change periodically as USPS rates change.	
U.P.S., Canadian & Foreign are extra.